LOVER My KING & I

A Spiritual Journey in Poetry

Esha Gabrielle
Johnson

First published in 2008

ISBN: 978-1-8383038-3-9

Cover Design & Layout by David Springer.

FOREWORD

This book in not just a collection of poems; it will take you to the heart of the Father. Meditate on each poem, prayer, words of encouragement and scripture and you will feel a new passion for God arise in your spirit.

Esha is a woman after God's heart, she writes out of the rich tapestry of her own life experiences. She was raised in the Caribbean and came to the UK to join her parents at the age of 8 years. As a child, she learnt to be seen and not heard, this led her to begin writing at the age of 9 years, as a way of finding her voice.

The poems have been written over a number of years at different stages of her journey. They display her humour, her pain, sensitivity and recovery, through the pen.

Use this in your own meditations and you too, will come to know the Lord in a deeper way as 'Your Lover and Your King'.

Sheila Hendley
Director Academy for Life UK

PREFACE

I believe my purpose here on earth is enabling others to see the creative beauty that God has placed within them. Encouraging others to see themselves as God sees them, a precious gem, they then become a catalyst to enriching other people's lives.

It is my hope that somewhere along these pages you will find moments of joy, laughter, peace, wonderment, and most of all, possibly you may shed a tear while you smile.

Before you embark on your journey with me through these pages, I want you to read this book of creative poetry and prayers as though they have been personally written for you. As you walk through the pages, don't rush, walk slowly, and sometimes walk real slow... Snail pace. Take time to savour every word. Reflect by reading between the lines, use your spiritual eyes to look deep and listen attentively to the Spirit within, to hear what is really being said. Allow your mind to search your heart, because in searching your heart, you will release your soul.

As we journey down the pathway of my heart, I will introduce you to my soul's desire, you probably already know Him, but it's okay if you don't. Come along anyway, you will enjoy meeting Him and He certainly wants to meet and get to know you.

To make this journey more intimate, insert you name in the spaces below, then read aloud. Let the words rest in the centre of your spirit.

Psalm 121

God's Divine Protection

When you put your trust in Him

………… will lift up ….. eyes unto the hills

From whence comes ….. help

…………'s help comes from the Lord

Which made heaven and earth

He will not suffer ………… 's foot to be moved

He that keeps ………… will not slumber

Behold He that keeps …………

Shall not slumber nor sleep

The Lord is …………'s keeper

The Lord is ………..'s shade upon ………..'s right hand

The sun shall not smite ………… by day

Nor the moon by night

The Lord shall preserve ………… from all evil

He shall preserve …………'s soul

The Lord shall preserve …………'s out going

And …………'s coming in from this time forth

And even for evermore.

Know that He who chose you from before the foundation of the world loves you with an everlasting love. He will never leave or forsake you!

From My Heart to Your Heart.

DEDICATED TO HIM

My Lover and My King
The Triune God
Father, Son and Holy Spirit
The One without Beginning or Ending
The First of all things
The Last in everything
The Alpha and Omega
The Omnipresent and Omnipotent One
The I Am that I Am
The all Seeing and all Knowing
The King of all kings
The Lord of all lords
The God above all gods
The One who sits upon the throne in the upper heavens
The Creator of all existence
To the Most High God
'YHWH'
MY Abba.

The earth is the Lord's, and the fullness thereof; the world, and they that dwell therein.
Psalm 24:1 KJV

And you shall love ADONAI you God with all your heart and with all your soul and with all your strength. These words, which I am commanding you today, are to be on your heart. You are to teach them diligently to your children, and speak of them when you sit in your house, when you walk by the way, when you lie down and when you rise up. Bind them as a sign on your hand, they are to be as a frontlet between your eyes, and write them on the door post of your house and on your gates...

Deuteronomy 6:5-9
Tree of Life Version

ADVICE

As a counselling practitioner, I am trained not to give advice. Ethically, a therapist should only ever guide people to make their own decisions. All good. This helps to keep both client and counsellor safe. This also is true outside the arena of my work. As I've ventured deeper into my profession and daily life, I'm learning to mind my business and leave people to make their own life choices; after all, as believers in Christ we have a responsibility to work out our own salvation with fear and trembling. HOWEVER! On this love journey, I am breaking all the rules...Good relevant biblical advice helps us to soul search and draw closer to God...

As iron sharpens iron so a person sharpens the countenance of his friend. Proverbs 27:17 TLV.

Some years ago, I went through a really dry, brittle season, *(must have been a long period of time),* when I just did not pray. I am not quite sure what was happening, but my prayer life was just non-existent. Not sure whether you have ever had a period in your life where you just functioned on auto-pilot? When you prayerlessly operate from day to day just expecting God to keep you, without any real thought about Him? Yep! Been there, done that!

WOW, Christianity without God-connection! As children of God we cannot afford to have prayerless faith. *Sounds real bad now I'm writing about it,* but it was what it was. The enemy is on a mission, his bow is pulled back far and the arrow is headed straight for us.

By the way, *I'm just gonna keep this book real simple; you won't need a dictionary. This is just friend-talk whilst walking on* *a journey with my, and hopefully, your King...*Anyway, back to the subject of prayer.

For ages I didn't pray, not because I couldn't, I just didn't bother. My advice to you is, do not take God for granted. **Warning:** He is sovereign, He is All-knowing. His eyes run to and from the earth. He sees and knows *yah business.* You may not be watching Him but He is certainly watching you. You can't just pick Him up and throw Him down as and when. That is not how it works; you cannot do lukewarm. You are either hot or cold, you cannot juggle Him; you are either for Him or against Him, but not both. Be very clear, He has a standard of holiness and without holiness you cannot see His spiritual vision and purpose for you.

Do not play games with God and expect Him to run to your aid when you are in trouble; that is called taking advantage. Sometimes we just need to fix-up. There must come a time in our lives when we make a conscious decision to serve God wholeheartedly, have a pure unadulterated relationship with Him, true intimacy, no wavering.

Have you ever heard God speak? My goodness! He does. I will never forget the day, *in the middle of my dry prayerless season,* when HE STOPPED ME IN MY TRACKS! Gee-whiz, gracious me! God speaks audibly, just like having a conversation with a friend, He speaks. I have heard preachers try to play it down about God speaking to people audibly, but that's their opinion. It was the second time I had heard His audible sound. You say, Esha, "How do you know it was God speaking to you?" Trust me when you hear God's voice, you know. You just know because it is like no other sound you have ever heard before.

There I was pottering around the kitchen and I heard...

"Esha, every day the enemy turns up before me to accuse you, where are you?"

Yeek! To say I was in a state of shock is an understatement. I was speechless. And no, I didn't drop on my knees and pray there and then, but I remember being numb for a long time! One thing I have learnt from my Jewish study bible is that, 'Shame is the gravest punishment.' Ancient Israel was a shame orientated society. *Thank God for Jesus.* It is shameful when we so easily disconnect and dishonour God through prayerlessness; we completely forget that our relationship with Him is a two-way interaction. We are often so dismissive of His deep desire for us and His pain when we reject Him.

'Shame is the gravest punishment!'

We often blame our inconsistent prayer lives on our busyness, but this is not always the case, because when we do have time we still chose not to pray and we find other things to occupy our minds. Sometimes it is just simply an attitude of *'I can't be bothered',* laziness. Therefore, time is not the issue. When we encounter difficulties, we pray, and once our situations are resolved, God goes on the back burner, until He is fished out again in desperation; used, misused and abused. I know this because that was my former routine until my encounter with the truth. So again, my advice to you, keep daily open communication with God. It is imperative that you show up in His presence every day; I cannot emphasise this enough. God knows your voice, so find your rhythm with Him by committing in prayer daily.

It is a privilege to have bare-faced opportunity to enter the throne room of heaven, *whenever.* You do not need clergy permission. It is free access through the Blood of Yeshua (Jesus).

I believe every child of God has a unique sound. No matter how many of His children are praying at the same time, in any language, in any culture, of any race, in any nation, God can distinguish our individual unique sound *(Psalm 19 v 3).* God knows, MY VOICE, YOUR VOICE! HE KNOWS MY SOUND, HE KNOWS YOUR SOUND, and when He does not hear your sound it saddens Him. It grieves the Holy Spirit when we choose to ignore the God who loved the world so much, He willingly gave up His Son as a sacrificial offering for us.

Back to the story!

There was the enemy turning up every day in the courts of heaven to accuse me of whatever, and I was not showing up to say *'boo'...Like I'm invincible and give myself the breath of life.* I totally dismissed who it was making intercession and defending me consistently, **FOR FREE!** What I really needed was a holy back-hand!

Since the day I heard the audible voice of God, I began to pray, and over the years, my prayer life has strengthened. The more I pray is the more He reveals Himself to me and the more I fall in love with Him. In fact, the very first thing I do when I wake up in the morning is blow my King a kiss...*that is my known heavenly signature.* The mere fact I wake up is enough to give Him thanks. Every night people go to sleep confident about their plans for tomorrow, but they never wake to see those plans materialise. No one is promised tomorrow.

Waking up is a gift! My God, He is my rock, He never sleeps or slumbers. He is my guardian at night and my daily covering. My advice again - draw close to God the Father and He will draw close to you. Seek Him early; never leave your home without inviting the Holy Spirit to participate in your day. He is your ultimate guide. He knows how to strategically take you around the enemy. Put your life in the hands of the God of heaven's armies. You only have today, and even this moment, you don't know about tomorrow. Do it now! Today is the day to PRAY! Today is the day to praise, worship and honour El Elyon, the Most High God.

Let the journey begin!

DAILY COVERING

Father of Creation, My King
I love You with all of my heart, all of my soul,
and all of my strength.

As I kneel in Your presence, I come to You in the Name of Your
Son, Yeshua, Jesus Christ as we know Him today
I come to You under the covering of the BLOOD that was shed
for me upon the cross at Calvary.
I come under the anointing of those blood-stained hands, blood-
stained feet and the piercing side of Your Son, Yeshua, the
Christ...Alleluia
I enter Your throne room with bold authority, through the
permission of the intercessory prayer continually made for me
by Your Son, Yeshua.
My, God, my Father, my King there is no one greater that
You my Creator
I exalt You for there is nobody like You Lord.

Lord look at me through the sacrificial Blood, let Your eyes of
compassion search me; where I have sinned and come short of
your glory please forgive me. This morning I ask You to create
in me a clean heart and a right spirit. Let the words I speak and
the thoughts of my mind be pleasing to you today.

Father, I come today to talk to You, to seek Your face.
I come to praise You, to lift up Your Name.
I come to be in Your presence where there is fullness of joy.
I come this morning to sharpen my sword;
ignite Your Word in me.
I come to let You secure my armour and tighten
my belt with Your truth.

I come that You can fasten my breastplate of righteousness to guard my heart and be in right standing with You.
I come to get my shoes prepared with the gospel of peace.
I come to rub my shield of faith upon Your royal garment; so as in the days of King Solomon it will shine with the fire of Your glory; well able to quench the fiery darts of the enemy.
I come so You can steady my helmet of salvation to keep my mind stayed on the beauty of Your Holiness
Lord, I have come that Your Holy Spirit can walk with my spirit today.
You are my divine protector. With You by my side nothing can befall me
I have come, like the woman with the issue of blood, to draw strength from You today. Today I come because I know with You as my director, I am able to stand against the plans of the enemy. As I walk down the road today, he will know... I'M NOT PLAYING...cross over...there is POWER, LOVE and a SOUND MIND in this child of the heavenly King...Back off.
Lord, I am Your ambassador in training. I am open to Your teaching, open to Your leading. Lord, my God and King, I need Your divine knowledge, wisdom and understanding to help me work effectively and worship You through my day. Teach me Your way. My desire is to know You; to be truly connected to You, whatever it takes. I quote Your word back to You; *John 4:24; God is a spirit: and they that worship Him must worship Him in spirit and in truth*. I want to be a true worshipper.

Lord, today I come to You, asking You to order my steps. Allow me today to be a light in someone's darkness.

I seal this prayer with the blood of My Lord and Saviour Yeshua the Christ.

Amen

MY LOVER, MY KING & I

Ignited, the passion of burning flames
Relished affections
An exquisite love affair
Between My Lover, My King and I.

Devoted desires, delighted tenderness
Sweetly caressed in graceful adoration
A romantic love affair
Between My Lover, My King and I

Hearts betrothed, interlocked souls
The cherished warmth of charmed embrace
An intense love affair
Between My Lover, My King and I

Pleasant aromas of idolised joy
Inflamed in the promise of divine destiny
An everlasting love affair
Between My Lover, My King and I.

"O Lord, God of Israel, there is no God like You, in heaven
or on earth keeping covenant and showing steadfast
love to your servants who walk before
You with all their hearts."
2 Chronicles 6:14 KJV

In the 21st century, scientists, assisted by government funds, have spent billions of pounds/dollars trying to establish how the world was formed. They have done umpteen experiments, visited the moon, sent satellites into space orbiting the planets, sent spaceships around the globe. To date, as far as I am aware, they are still looking and making many frivolous claims. More world governments, more scientists and evolutionists are running around, concluding some logical explanation, all wanting to outdo each other, put their country on the map of discovery and world victory.

The Church of God can give them the answer
in one sentence.
Genesis chapter one and verse one
Proclaims:
(Drum roll please)
IN THE BEGINNING GOD CREATED THE HEAVEN AND THE EARTH!
Told you: **ONE** sentence.
Case closed!
My KING! HE IS AWESOME!

DO YOU KNOW HIM?

Do you know Him?
Let me introduce you to my friend
My Lover and My King
My life source, my most intimate soul mate.

Do you know Him?
The architect of my life, author and
finisher of my faith
He who from before the foundation of the world
Organised me in His thoughts
He who knew me before He formed me
in my mother's womb
He whose spirit I am saturated in.

Do you know Him?
My knight in shining armour?
The One with the sharp two-edged sword
The sword that cuts the debris from my life
He who loves me beyond measure.

Do you know Him?
Ever heard of, or met the perfect gentleman?
I know Him! He's My Lover and My King!
He is like no other man
Will never use, reject and discard me
My divine protector has never a cause to hurt me
Chooses never to leave my side
Day after day, night after night
Hour after hour, moment by moment.

Do you know Him?
My Lover and My King
He who pulled the thorns from my inner being
Wrapped His light around my feet
Straightened the pathway of my life
Healed my wounds and alleviated the
pain of my broken heart
He who erased the memories of my suffering
Dried my tears and still refuses to let me go.

Do you know Him?
Through His eyes I am His amazing masterpiece
So, who am I not to consider myself blessed?
Is He not my outstanding grace?
Am I not His ultimate joy?
Such was, and is His love for me.
He died and stands in resurrected glory for me!
His presence is created light surrounding my soul
and transcending through my veins to give me life.

Do you know Him?
The One who keeps me through His
all sufficient grace
Whose mercies are everlasting!
Him who upholds me with His righteousness
He whose blood purifies my inner me, night and day
He who hides me from the wrath of the Holy Father
For, does He not set up a standard
against my accuser?
Is He not my barrister in the courts of heaven?
Is He not defending my every accusation, with
His blood-stained hands?
My question is:
Do you know Him?

Again I say,
Do you know Him?
NO! Not about Him!
Do you know Him?
My breath, my lifeline
The one who woke me up this morning
Who turned my dead into living!
He whose mercies were new this morning
He whose faithfulness is great right NOW!
For His forgiveness is over me right NOW!

Do you know Him?
My Lover My King
Who searches my thoughts and knows
the condition of my heart
He who is my protective armour and shield
Whose scent is an aroma of sacrificial Blood.

Do you know Him?
My life-living water from the well that never runs dry
My overflowing cup of grace filled with
goodness everyday.

Do you know Him?
He who orders my steps and strengthens
my crooked path
Who cushions my fall and picks me up
Steadies my feet and directs my way.
Do you know Him?
He who catches my frown and throws me a smile
He knows me more than I know me
My wholeness is in Him.

Do you know Him?
The light of my salvation
He in whom I put all my trust
He who is the glory of my strength
He whose name I honour and adore.

Do you know Him?
He who opens my doors of light and
closes my used doors of despair
My shepherd who cause me to lie down
in the harmony of peace
He who restores my life and covers
me with the joy of hope
He who keeps my mind stayed upon
things that are lovely
He who reminds me of things that are
pure and kind and just
The restorer of my soul
For His steadfast love never ceases.

Do you know Him?
The One who in the grave death could not control
For He is the risen King sitting in triumph
He is where all of my help comes from
For when the dark in me saw His light, it let me go
His grace is sufficient to keep me.

Again I ask!
Do You Know Him?
He whose faithfulness is my body armour and shield.

MY LOVER & MY KING
I AM COMPLETE IN HIM!

And this is the way to have eternal life
To know You, the only true God, and Jesus Christ,
the one You sent to earth. John 17:3 KJV

When God sets you up!

I find the story of Queen Esther both fascinating and enchanting. It is like a biblical fairy-tale, from rags to riches. The girl gets her man and lives happily ever after; from ordinary to extraordinary. Reminds me that with God, anything is possible.

As the saying goes, "Luck is when preparation meets opportunity" (Roman philosopher Seneca).

Esther must have felt devastated when she was forcibly taken from her home and loved ones. In biblical times she would not have been given a choice; you did not refuse the king. For all we know, she may have been engaged to someone else in her Jewish community, so taking her on demand must have been heart-wrenching. Nevertheless, she was obedient in taking on the challenge in her duty of preparation to meet the king. Eventually, after many months and much patience, she was called, chosen, and appointed to the most prestigious position as Queen of Persia. However, the journey to the palace and becoming queen were only just the beginnings of a more comprehensive mission, where she ended up risking her life to save her people. In biblical times the custom was, if you were not summoned by the king, you did not come into his presence. This rule extended to Queen Esther - there were no exceptions. So, when she breeched protocol and appeared before the king without his permission, she risked losing her life; she was staring at death. In the story, (please read it) Esther 4:16, she tells her uncle Mordecai...

"I will go to the king, even though it is against the law, and if I perish, I perish."

When I was doing my counselling training, I heard someone make a statement that has stuck with me until this day. It was: ***'The darkest part of the room is where the door is!'*** My interpretation of this is that sometimes we have to come out of our comfort zones and face our fear; dark does not know it's dark until it meets light. Facing our fears help shape our focus in both character and personality. Most importantly, it gives us the strength to move forward and progress, thus obtaining a favourable outcome.

Esther had a desired outcome. She had an extra special relationship with the King. He was bedazzled by both her mannerism and her beauty. His heart connected with her heart in unspoken passion, hence he held out his sceptre to bid her come. The impression I get from the story is that the king did not just love Esther, he was in love with her. She had an anointed presence which he could not refuse.

God will always ensure that you find favour on the other side to the door that He opens for you.

The story of Esther I believe, epitomises the passion Christ has for His church. Esther appeared before the king afraid and gained acceptance and victory for her people. Christ overcame His fear in the garden of Gethsemane and gained exceptional victory for His people on the cross. Their darkest moments became the light that shattered the darkness.

AS ONLY A LOVER CAN

Your sceptre stretched... I accept
Draw me to Your warm embrace
My soul I surrender to You
My heart, take rest in Your bosom
Your eyes as flames of fire
Truly, I am enchanted

My Lover...My King
Bid me to come
Your sceptre I hold
I bow to You...to You
To You alone I bow
My emotions in response to Your touch
The quietness of Your breath
Blow Your gentle kiss in my ear
O the blessings of being welcomed in Your presence

My Lover...My King
I draw close to You my King
Stretch Your sceptre and draw close to me
I am mesmerised by Your expressive warmth
The glory of Your holiness...I behold
The reflection of Your royalness...my eyes penetrate
The transparency of Your truth captivates my mind
My heart pounds in reverence of Your acceptance
You my Love...Yes! You alone...
My Lover...My King...Capture me
As only a Lover can.

And it was so, when the King saw Esther the queen standing in the court, that she obtained favour in his sight, and the king held out to Esther the golden sceptre that was in his hand. So Esther drew near, and touched the top of the sceptre.
Esther 5:2 KJV

IN AWE

The Great I AM
Illustrated glory of my life
Lover of my soul
Joy of my salvation
Director of my destination
Restorer of my life
Majesty of holiness
I am in Awe

His imperial Royalness
In honour I bow before You
I have sought You and found You
NO!, I will not let You go
As You pass by I reached out and touched
Oh! The transcendent power of Your virtue
I am in Awe

Turn Lord and see my grip on Your hem
The change!
NO!, I will not let You go
On You I am learning to lean
My exalting hold will not let go
My adoring grasp is tightly firm
In You Lord I am securely anchored
I am humbled Lord that You stopped and took me in
Lord, I am in awe of You
I AM IN AWE!

With my whole heart I have sought thee: O let me
not wonder from thy commandments
Psalms 119:10 KJV

I have come to realise that when I entered the personal space of Yeshua the Son of God, I was no longer my own; I forfeited all my rights to do my own thing when I placed my life in His hands.

Therefore, if anyone be in Christ, he is a new creature; old things have passed away; Behold all things have become new.
2 Corinthians 5:17 KJV

MY INTEGRITY

Lord reach deep into my soul
Expose any hidden darkness within me
Cause me to wash my heart from evil
When rebellion wars inside my members
Help me to maintain my integrity
By staying in control
When my mouth is tempted to curse
Help me to maintain my integrity
By bringing my tongue under subjection
When my feet are straggling the path of destruction
Help to maintain my integrity
By guiding me on the pathway of life
When I make a fist in moments of anger
Help me to maintain my integrity
By holding my peace
Lord, when I am tempted to defile my body
Help me to maintain my integrity
By reminding me that my body is your temple
When my mind becomes entrenched with thoughts
of bitterness
Help me to maintain my integrity
By reaching down to the depth of my bowels
And find the spirit of forgiveness
Lord, whenever I consider presumptuousness
Help me to maintain my integrity
And uphold Your righteousness.

Create in me a clean heart, O God; and
renew a right spirit within me.
Psalm 51:10 KJV

MY LOVE

My King
Take Your place upon the pinnacle of my soul
Today My Love
Proudly sit upon the throne in my heart
Come now My Lover
Reflect the light of Your Holiness central in my mind
For the centre of...Me...Belongs to You.

Only Your spirit my Holy King
Can enter and sit on the throne of my heart
Only You My Love
Can cross the boundaries and indwell in my secret place
Only You can uproot and replant
Today my King
Come in, come in, come in
Come in and take Your place in this temple
Sit in my created space purposed for You.

Stay my Lord, stay
Stay, for in You I nurture my soul.

Let my soul live, and it shall praise thee;
and let your judgments help me.
Psalms 119:175 KJV

I often wonder why most people wait until the beginning of a new year to reflect on their lives. I reflect every day. Self-observation is an ongoing process in my life. I don't need an occasion, such as death, funerals, break-ups or breakdowns, to pause for thought. I spend my life in reflective thought getting to know me, sometimes too much thought. I really do not need anyone to point out my flaws or faults. I am totally aware of my process, the changes and improvements I need to make. I talk to God, LOADS, about me. He knows and I know.

I have arranged and rearranged my internal furniture so many times in my life, to the extent where I became so frustrated and dissatisfied with myself. It just didn't look good enough. The sofa in my heart wasn't comfortable - it wasn't perfect, and try as I might, I just could not get it to look or feel perfect. So I prayed to My King - handed me to Him. I surrendered all my self-discontentment to His Holy Spirit and left Him to do the cleaning and polishing. I left Him to repair some broken stuff, throw out large bags of rubbish and position the furniture how He saw fit. Mind you, I did try to hold on to some well glued down baggage, but on reflection, I just found it easier to let go and leave it to Him. True to His word, He has taken me from errors of darkness into His marvellous light.

ERRORS OF DARKNESS

Oh wretch that I am
Lord, I am not deserving of You
Lord, O my God
Do not cast me away
I pray, my Lord, my God
Let me taste of Your goodness
Let my feet declare the light of Your word
Let the meditation of my heart
Cause You to smile
Let the thoughts of my mind
Cause Your brow to rise.

My Lord, God and King
Deliver me from the enemy
of self-righteousness
Let me continually be mindful
of my doings
Let my motives never be to exalt
myself above You
Deliver my soul from iniquity
Then I can be free to worship You
In spirit and in truth.

My God and Saviour
Lord of my life
Help me to be so in tuned
with the presence of Your glory
So much so Lord, so intertwined
There will be no room for errors of darkness.

Search me O God, and know my heart. Examine me,
and know my anxious thoughts: and see if there be any offensive
way within me, and lead me in the way everlasting.

Psalm 139:23-24

Tree of Life Version

ACADEMY FOR LIFE

Psalm of exaltation

Because you have made the Lord
Which is my refuge, even the Most High
Your habitation.
Psalm 91:9

Every day Lord
I allow You access into my being
You! The Most High God
Today walk freely in my body
You are my refuge
Inhabit where You will.

I exalt YOU my Lord! My King!
I exalt YOU! You alone I worship
I exalt YOU far above all gods
There is none other like YOU
Today and every day I magnify YOU
Because of who YOU are
I set my sight upon YOU.

Because of who You are
I make You my habitation
I make room in my soul
For Your indwelling spirit
I move myself aside
I get ready my temple
Come Holy Spirit
Take residence inside me
Today!

Like King David
I abide under the shadow
Of Your wings
and in the secrecy of Your Holiness
Today Lord, make me a part
of Your Academy for life.

From My heart Lord to Your heart

The word of the Lord declares that
When we ask it will be given to us
When we diligently seek Him we
will find Him
When we knock on His door, it will be
opened to us
To be like Him is to fervently chase
after His righteousness.

DEAR JESUS

**Let a tear drop You cried
for mankind at Calvary
fall upon my heart.
Let the blood You shed
massage my soul.**

**Wash me in the mercy of Your grace.
Pull down every stronghold or anything
in my life which exalts itself above You.
Inject my mind with thoughts of forgiveness.**

**Oh God, cause me to engage in the
passion of intimacy I so desire with You.
Tune my ears to the music of Your righteousness.
Open my eyes to the light of Your glory.
Incline my mouth and the voice of my breath
to utter words of wisdom, blessings and kindness.
Allow the totality of my being
to actively demonstrate Your grace.**

**Holy Spirit, teach my character to embrace
the humbleness of obedience.
Allow the radiance of Your beauty
to shine through my life
so that others may see and glorify Your Name.**

*As the deer longs for streams of water,
so I long for You, O God.
Psalms 42:1NLT*

Body, Spirit and Soul, in that order...

God took the soil from the ground, shaped it to form a man in His own image - put His mouth to the man's mouth and blew His Spirit into his limp body, creating a soul which caused the man to come to life.

This morning as I sit here writing, I am taking time to breathe slowly; IN...One...Two...Three...OUT...One...Two...Three. I am mindfully taking note of the functioning of my body with each breath, meditating on the goodness of God, giving my King thanks for His immense power and supernatural Spirit in this earthen vessel, that He gifts to me every morning. ***I am in tears now!***

What a mighty God we serve. **STOP READING**...Just stop for a moment and BREATHE DEEP! Take time to notice your breathing.

Do you realise you are the breath of God?
If yes, shout...

Halleluyah!

In Lamentations 3:22-23 the Prophet Jeremiah, crying in distress said:

"It is because of the LORD'S mercies that we are not consumed, because His compassions fail not. They are new every morning: great is thy faithfulness."

The breath in the body you are living in belongs to God. If He chooses to allow death to take you right now, His Breath, meaning His spirt, will return to Him. The absence of God's spirt is a dead body; hence our body is His temple to be kept holy. I heard Maya Angelou, in an interview, make a statement that I hold onto dearly. I paraphrase, it went something like this;

> *"There should be a place inside everyone where only God is able to go. No one else is allowed in that space but God."*

Let me be very clear here, whether or not people choose to serve God, the creator of all living things, it is His breath that is within them (It is God's). Whatever choice a person makes in life, good or bad, they must be aware they are on God's time. The breath they breathe is God's breath. No scientist is able to create breath NONE! God gives life and He takes life.
1 Samuel 2:6

RUACH

Ruach
The breath of God
Like a gentle wind He blows
The softness of His Shekinah Glory
An overflow of His Spirit raining down upon me,
Racing through my veins and feeding my life within.

Ruach
The breath of God
Like the calming of a summer's breeze
Sharing the elegance of an evening sky
The warmth of compassion
His grace and mercies flowing me through.

Ruach
The breath of God
A soothing of my mind
With His fragrance of hope
Inhaling deeply through my nostrils
A gentle breeze surrounding me
Energising and nourishing my soul.

Ruach
With Your breath in me I embrace You my Lord!
With Your breath in me, a reverent kiss I blow to You my King!
Mmmmmm!

BREATHE!

And the Lord God formed man of the dust of the ground, and breathed into his nostrils the breath of life; and man became a living soul.
Genesis 2:7 KJV

I am absolutely fascinated with angels. In my studies I have learnt that there are nine ranks of angels, the seraphim having the highest position in heaven. Seraphim is plural and is derived from the Hebrew word 'saraph' which means 'to burn.' They are fiery and in total reverence of God. Isaiah 2:6 tells us they have six wings. With two they cover their face, with two they cover their feet and with two they fly around the throne proclaiming the Father's Holiness: *"Holy, holy, holy is the Lord Almighty; the whole earth is full of His glory"* Isaiah 6:3. It is said that Seraphim serve as God's agents of purification, they were responsible for cleansing Isaiah's sins, by touching his tongue with hot coal from heaven, before he began his ministry.

I think my inquisitive mind for angels began some years ago, after listening to Jessie Duplantis talking about a vision he had of going to heaven and meeting the seraphim. As he recalled his vision he said, and again I paraphrase:
"I watched them fly around the throne continuously, and after watching a while I stopped one of them and said, "Don't you ever get tired of flying around the throne? You must have been doing this for years." To his and my astonishment, the seraphim answered and said ***"NO I never get tired because every time I fly around the throne I learn something new."***

When I heard that statement I thought, my goodness, NOOO! Our God is amazing - you simply cannot out-learn Him. Just imagine, throughout eternity we will be gaining new knowledge about Him every day. He will never run out of being! As the young people would say: *How cool is that!*

Just take a moment to fully comprehend what the seraphim said! I don't know about you, but I serve an unending God, His existence will never come to an end! There is NOBODY like my KING! Bless You Lord.

The next poem is how I am feeling about Him today, right now!

TODAY!

Again, I realise Lord, how wonderful You are to me
My soul cries out in worship to You
My heart burns with passion for You
Today.
Allow Your Holy Spirit in me to draw me close to You.
My undivided attention is focussed on You Lord
Light up my life with the fire of Your glory
Today.
Like the four and twenty elders falling
down before You
My soul cries Holy Holy Holy
Lord God Almighty
Exalted in splendour upon Your throne
How precious is the newness of Your sound
How majestic in authority.
Today.
Like the Seraphim flying around Your throne
My soul cries Holy Holy Holy to God Most High
There is nobody like YHWH
I celebrate You my King
Today.
Lord let Your nostrils inhale my praise
Let it be a nourishing sweet-smelling
savour to Your Spirit
Let me be worthy of the blessings You
bestow upon me each day.
Let me be worthy of the price You paid for me!

For Adonai is a great God and a great King above all gods,
In His hands are the depths of the earth.
Psalms 95:3-4 TLV

Hearing Ears

Oh Lord, open my ears, to hear
The stillness of Your quietness.
Open my ears to the silence of Your breath.
Open my ears to the voice of Your heartbeat and the life of Your blood.
Engage me in Your spectacular glory
and the dynamics of Your presence.
Open my soul to the grace of Your love.
Let everything within me never cease to praise, to honour and magnify You.

In You, ADONAI, have I taken my refuge:
Let me never be put to shame.
In Your righteousness, deliver me. Turn Your ear
to me, rescue me quickly.
Be a rock or refuge for me, a stronghold for my deliverance.
Psalm 31:2-3 Tree of Life Version.

Do you like writing?

I love my pen. I love any excuse to write, especially about my Lover & my King. I am in my element and totally at peace when I am writing about Him. It is what I enjoy doing most in life. I write in all kinds of notebooks, scraps of paper, lined or plain. As He the Holy Spirit gives me a thought, I write. I write on anything I can find, I have even written on toilet paper on my bedside table when I couldn't find my note book. One night I woke up, and in my eagerness to capture the words flowing in my thoughts I wrote on my notepad in the dark. I must find something to write on about my King. I have umpteen notebooks all about Him. He really knows my heart. With my pen I can tell Him anything without feeling ashamed, embarrassed, belittled, silly, criticised, or judged. He loves me just as I am. He loves me when I am right and even when my errors make me wrong. I truly love my King. He is my soul's desire, my heart, my life source, my breath, my mind, my victory, my hope, my blessed assurance, my mind light, my darkness repellent, my transformation, my victory, my root of righteousness and justice, my spiritual defender. I love my pen especially writing about my King! My pen is expressive and knows how to draw His creative beauty from my inner spirit. My pen allows me to speak, it knows how to search His Spirit in me and find His joy to feed my mind and keep me centred on His poetic voice in me for His Holy Spirit is Master Spoken Artist.

My Lover & My King
Original Spoken Word

In the beginning was the WORD and the WORD was
with God and the WORD was God.
John 1:1 KJV

HE IS WORTHY

When you know the love of the King
The One who died to transform you
When you know the love of the Christ
The One who conquered death, took the keys and arose
When you know the love of the victorious One
He, Him, who loves you far beyond your expectations
He, who laid down is life for YOU, His friend
YOU, His son, YOU, His daughter, YOU, His child
When you know that you were the foetus of His mind
Fearfully and wonderfully made in His image
When you know that your Lover is in the presence of the King
Your Lover, seated on His right hand, with Holy blood!
Making intercession for your bridal entrance
When you know, that you know, that you know
The love of the Saviour, Son of the living God
When your heart contacts with His heart
When you experience Him in spirit and in truth
When you know the authenticity, the transparency, the pureness

OF HIS AGAPE
Then you know HE IS WORTHY to be praised.

I will exalt You, my God, the King, and I will bless Your Name forever and ever.
Every day I will bless You, and praise Your Name forever and ever.
Great is ADONAI, and greatly to be praised.
His greatness is unsearchable
Psalm 145:1-3 Tree of Life Version

Have you ever met an overly religious person? *Good gracious me, "What's wrong with people?"* Christians who are so heavenly minded they are no earthly good - they never do anything wrong, and everything you do is a problem. *Man,* they are so righteous, they never question God about anything.

Sometimes we just need to real-up...I am very real with my God. I have come to realise that if I am real with Him, then He is real with me. He can correct me when I am wrong or give insight to my ignorance. God is all knowing, He already knows my truth, He knows my thoughts, as King David wrote in Psalms 139:1-2 NLT

O Lord, You have examined my heart and know everything about me You know when I sit down and stand up. You know my thoughts even when I'm far away

You see, God knows me. He knows who I am. He hears and knows the content of my mind. He is attuned with my thoughts even before I think them. So, if I have a question on my heart, why am I hiding it? Why am I walking around in heaviness instead of expressing my feelings to Him? What is the point in Him being my God if I can't be honest with Him? The amount of times I got into trouble at church for my difference of opinion.
I asked God a question that may not be important to anyone else, but it was really important to me. I asked Him about my race. I wanted to know why as a race of people we experienced so much hatred from the rest of the world. I needed to know because sometimes the hatred gets exhausting. Some days I get tired and worn out! *I just want to live.* Sometimes the pain I see my race in is overbearing. It may sound childish and although I have been a Christian for many years, I was a little curious as to whether He loved my race the same as others. I wanted to

know what it was that our ancestors had done so wrong that we were being punished. I found myself reminding God about His Abrahamic promises. I remember saying to Him, "When You saved me I was adopted into Your family, the promises of Abraham are extended to me, plus adopted children are special children; adopted children are chosen. Your word says you are no respecter of persons so why does the suffering of my people seem more severe than any other race?
I wanted to know why.

In my anger and frustration I have found myself shouting and screaming at God and having to apologise. *...Oops, good Christians never do that?* Thank You Lord for Yeshua, and thank you Yeshua for being the best barrister ever, in the courts of heaven. I know the case against me sometimes takes a lot of Blood. *You can stop holding yuh breath and exhale...* I am serious when I say I am grateful to my King, Lord and Saviour...love Him loads.

HUGE BREATH! This is book about love, but can I get a little deeper with this subject?
I think in any culture or race, even as a child of God, if you feel consistently attacked, if you are not vigilant, you begin to entertain some real ungodly thoughts and the same perpetrated hatred others have towards you begin to creep in.
God works in mysterious ways!

Following my meltdown with God, I remember going into my local bank. It was packed and as I stood waiting in the queue/ line, in an instant, the entire bank just transformed before my eyes. Everything slowed down and everyone disappeared; all I saw was floating souls, literally floating souls. It was a vision I will never forget, just souls. 'God Sees Souls.' I can't tell you what happened next. I just remembering walking out of the bank, astounded. It was as though I had been transported to another world and back in seconds. 'DO NOT' tell me there is no God. My roots are too deep in Him; I saw what I saw. Be careful what you ask God for; choose your question wisely and prepare yourself for an unexpected answer. *As I am writing this, I am reminding myself that the evil against my race has nothing to do with God.*

Ephesians 6:12, clearly states, 'For we wrestle not against flesh and blood but against principalities, against powers, against rulers of darkness in this world, against spiritual wickedness in high places'.

Strange how we can go to church for many years, read the bible, listen to sermons over and over again without fully comprehending the word of God, until He gives you a meaningful revelation.

My King is a God of love. He is interested in all races, all nations, all people and languages. He is interested in every ounce of human existence, equality and justice. We are all His children, no matter how we choose to think or behave. None of us gets away with anything, *'For it is written vengeance is mine, I will repay, saith the Lord. Romans 12:19 NLT*

More advice:
If you have a WHY question to ask God, ask Him. Even if you are a little afraid of the answer, still ask. He already knows what's on your mind. Unlike some parents who tire and become weary when their three-year-old goes through their WHY stage of development, God never gets tired of His children talking to Him or even getting mad with Him sometimes. He welcomes our curiosity. Our questions help us develop knowledge, wisdom and understanding. More importantly, we become engaged in a greater intimacy with our King in realising His Love for us.

BEYOND THE RACES

"DO you know Him?
Unconditional LOVE; "Do you know Him?"
He is passionate about mankind.
He eradicates the dominance of hatred.
He sees beyond the races.
He embraces all cultures
He knows no colour line.
All life is His breath
His throne sits upon the foundation of
RIGHTEOUSNESS and JUSTICE
He sees all, He knows all
He walks the earth without boundaries.
The world...All...Allllll...territory is His.
His nature is to impart harmony...execute judgement!
Again I say; "Do you know Him?"
His name is Agape!

After this I beheld, and lo, a great multitude, which no man could number, of all nations, and kindreds, and people and tongues, stood before the lamb, clothed with white robes, and palms in their hands.
Revelations 7:9 KJV

I find it interesting, how so often, the weather dictates what sort of day we have. We change our minds according to the weather. We dress to suit the weather. We alter our moods and feelings to reflect the weather. If it's sunny we are pleasant, lighted hearted and have a great day. If it rains, we have a depressing day. If it's cold we can hardly move, and good grief, if it snows, life just comes to a standstill! *"I Isn't Going Nowhere."*

I truly believe that as you lose your youth you get wiser. Notably, as I am growing older, I am beginning to enjoy every God given moment of my life. I refuse to let the weather control my day. I encourage you to embrace your life, come rain, snow or sunshine. God never promised you tomorrow.

The DAY

You are the Day...Not the weather.
Each morning you arise is proof that you are the Day.
The night is darkness, a reminder to rest.
The night is the closed chapter of the Day.
The night signifies the soundness of sleep, unconscious, without awareness.
The Day signifies life, another breath
to rejoice in the Lord.
"This is the Day that the Lord has made".
You are the Day...
The weather should not determine what
sort of day you have because
You are the Day.
Whatever the weather, the Day can
change the atmosphere.
In the midst of rain, there can be sunshine.
On a cold winter morning, there can be warmth.
In slippery snow, there can be balance.
In the blazing sun, there can be shade.
In blustery wind, there can be shelter.
In a raging storm, there can be calm.
On a dull dark afternoon, there can be light.
You are the Day.
The Day is more than a conqueror;
Its confidence makes every goal achievable.
The Day will brighten any circumstance.
The brilliance of the Day can change and
overcome any obstacle.
If the Day is positive and thankful,
it will command the weather.

Why art thou cast down O my soul? And why art thou disquieted within me? Hope thou in God: for I shall yet praise him, who is the health of my countenance, and my God.
Psalm 42:11KJV

In my work I meet so many people, young and matured, who are traumatised with what life has thrown at them and they just want out. They are either angry, anxious, depressed, have feelings of uselessness, fear of failure, without any real direction in life. These are my favourite clients. I just love the challenge of helping them to explore and make sense of their world. I take pleasure is helping them to find and give expression to who they really are; finding their self-worth and discovering the gems inside of them. It's sheer satisfaction sitting in observational wonder at the look of awe on their faces, as they come into realisation of their creativity and purpose. The elation of having someone listening to them, hearing them, not judging them. Someone not only accepting them for who they are, but enabling them to put value on themselves, and then taking them from nothing to priceless value. Then watching them leave the room transformed...I LOVE MY WORK!

It's great to know who I AM! Daughter of the Most High!

My Daddy is a King!

If the Creator of heaven and earth, the everlasting One, who called everything into being - if He is capable of giving and taking life, is passionate about me and accepts me for who I am, then what do I care about what you think!
Lord I am so happy and grateful for Your unfailing love towards me.

It is better to trust in the Lord than to put confidence in man.
Psalm 118: 8 KJV

PROMISED QUEEN

I am so blessed to be promised
I am gifted to earth
I am a promised Queen
Called according to His purpose
I am the hidden treasure planted in my mother's womb.
He, My King, He predestined me before creation
It was He who called me into being
Loved me from the beginning
I am an invaluable gem...Precious!
Even before He lit up the darkness
And separated the waters from dry land
He, My King, thought of me.
I am gifted to the atmosphere of life
I am a promised Queen
Crowned with favour
Here to reign in my space
Set apart in this earthen vessel
Wonderfully made
Original blueprint of me.
Coded inner creativity from the treasure chest of heaven
I am a shining diamond, an immaculate priceless artwork
Designed by the thoughts of My King...NO mistakes
No! I am not a mistake
I am here by His spoken desire
According to His wilful purpose
I am so grateful to be living my promise
I am gifted to earth perfected by grace
I am seed rooted in depth, the blossoms of potential
I am a promised Queen!
Crowned with loving kindness, His greatness
and tender mercies.

Moreover, whom He predestined, these He also called:
Whom He called, these He also justified;
and whom He justified these He also glorified
Romans 8:30 NKJV.

MY AMAZING GRACE
WHO IS HE?

My Amazing Grace
Do you know Him?

My righteousness, my happiness
My peace of mind, the rock of my salvation.

My Amazing Grace
Do you know Him?

My faith, my joy, my hope,
My pleasure forever more.

My Amazing Grace
Do you know Him?

My goodness, my mercy
My strength, my comforter
Strong and mighty is He.

My Amazing Grace
Do you know Him?

My heart's desire,
My dwelling place
Director of my soul.

WHO IS HE?

My Amazing Grace
Do you know Him?

My Prince of peace, my help
My shield, my defender
My deliver, in Him do I trust.

MY AMAZING GRACE
DO YOU KNOW HIM?

The closer I get to my King is the more I realise the need to change. The purity of His love, His astounding passion for me! I've given up trying to understand the Great I Am and His Amazing Grace for me. I resign myself and say:

NAKED BEFORE YOU I STAND!

NAKED I STAND BEFORE HIM.

Naked I stand before Him
Nothing to hide
Nothing to declare
Naked I can stand before Him, I can.
Nothing precious I have to lose
Much in His presence I have to gain.

All seeing all knowing is He
Free is He to search my inward being
Eyes as torch lights, the cracks He observes
Every dark place a light is shone
Nothing to hide
Nothing to declare
Naked I can, before Him I stand.

In my chamber He's free to roam
Access never denied
Door never closed
My inner being examine He can.
Freedom to change or rearrange
Nothing to hide
Nothing to declare
Naked before Him I stand.

Do you know that your bodies are temples of the
Holy Spirit, who is in you; whom you have received from God?
You are not your own: You were bought at a price.
Therefore, honour God with your bodies.
1Corinthians 6:19-20 NIV

My Lover is the Truth, therefore, can I take one minute of this journey of love to be truthful with you - is that okay? Again, I'm being real. You know, as a child of the King, there are times when I feel out of control, my flesh is at war with my spirit because I am vexed. Take for instance, when I am driving and some nutcase wants to kiss my bumper, or squeeze pass when there's no room, or beep me for something that's not my fault - ever been in that situation? These are times when I don't feel like being nice. The Spirit of God instructs me to calm down, but my flesh is saying, 'wind your window down and tell him to get lost'. In heated rage, which voice do you think I listen to? Yep! I put my trust in myself because it makes me feel better. WRONG!

Thank God for Jesus!

The next poem is an example of needing to keep your eyes continually upon the Lord, asking Him for a daily covering. It's the importance of renewing our minds daily, a daily repentance, a daily cleansing from the flesh. You know why? I don't know what I would do if the Lord rejected me. I would be totally lost without Him. When I consider the emptiness King Saul felt when God removed His spirit from him, the mental torment, the emotional trauma must have been unbearable.

No, Noo, Noooo absolutely NO! I hear King David and I totally agree. Lord, whatever You do *(Lord have mercy)* PLEASE, don't take Your spirit away from me.

Cast me not away from Your presence; take
not Your Holy Spirit from me.
Psalm 51:11KJV

LOST WITHOUT YOU!

Don't leave me
Please don't shut me out
Don't take your spirit from me
Even when the me in me
Knows I've behaved badly
Don't leave me
I'm lost without YOU.

In those times when I refuse to hear
I close my eyes, pretend You're not there
Turn my back, engage in presumptuous sin
Run back to You when things go wrong
Even then don't leave me
I'm lost without YOU

Despite my temperament, my stubbornness
My deliberateness, disobedience, out of control
When I like the me in me, and the me feels it doesn't need You
When I believe my ways are better than Your ways
When You knock and self-will shuts You out
When in trouble I run back in desperation
Don't leave me
I'm lost without You.

Please, please, please
Don't leave me
Don't ever take Your Spirit away from me
Life is not worth living without You
I know You know that I know You know
I'm lost without You.

Trust in the Lord with all your heart; and lean not on your own understanding. In all your ways acknowledge Him, and He will direct your paths.
Proverbs 3:5-6 KJV

Do you love gardens? I do!

I can sit for ages observing nature. If you have been blessed with a garden, look out of your window right now! What condition is your garden in? Is it overgrown and full of weeds? Are there any suckers suffocating the plants? Do the trees need felling? Does the lawn need mowing? Do the plants need pruning or re-potting, are the roots deep enough for their continual growth? Does the soil need turning over and fertilising? Does the path need sweeping? Is the shed falling down? Does the fence need repairing to make it more secure? Are the plants situated in the right places? Have you got any fruit trees? Are the fruits on the trees edible? Can the Beloved pick and eat them? Is your garden beautiful and full of vibrant colours? Is it a peaceful place for thought and mediation?
Is your garden ready for the presence of the King?
Or does it need some urgent attention?

The Songs of Solomon, I believe, is a great illustration of divine love. A love between two passionate souls. A Lover who is not afraid to express the intensity of His affection to His beloved. A spiritual communion between the heavenly bridegroom, Christ, and His bride, the church. In chapter 4:16, one lover, besotted, expresses love to the other:

"Awake, O north wind; and come, thou south; blow upon my garden, that the spices thereof may flow out. Let my beloved come into His garden, and eat His pleasant fruits".

Sorry but sometimes the Psalms only really sound poetically expressive in the King James Version.

The intense love and careful detailed illustration of beauty, passion, and perfection in Songs of Solomon reminds me that Jesus is going to present His bride to His Father, the King, absolutely PERFECT. His preparation is unimaginable; He is leaving no stone unturned in making sure that the brilliance of His bride will put the sun out of business. Right now, He is working night and day to accomplish that perfection.

'He did this to present her to Himself as a glorious church without spot or wrinkle or any other blemish. Instead, she will be holy without fault.' Ephesians 5:27 NLT

I am really fussy about my garden. I'm agitated when my lawn looks overgrown or the flowers look withered. I'm never satisfied until it looks tidy. I love gardening TV programmes, how a designer can take an unkempt backyard and transform it into something stunning.

Can you remember how your life was before your transformation? But God! Only He can make beauty from ashes. Gardens are symbolic for growth, pleasure and delight; it's like an image of the soul in perfect peace. The Holy Spirit takes delight in taking up residence in the garden of our hearts.

THE GARDEN OF MY HEART

In the garden of my heart I plant all kinds of roses
Colours of the rainbow signifying my love for my King
An array of beauty, a reminder of His love for me.

Yellow...
A symbol of joy the delight of our friendship

Red...
His everlasting love, His passion;
my romantic need for Him

White...
His loyalty towards me, His purity and
comeliness; my reverence for Him

Pink...
The elegance of His grace; my happiness, my appreciation, my
admiration of Him

Orange...
He's the ultimate desire of my soul;
His enthusiasm for me

Purple...
How majestic is He, clothed in royal
apparel; a King indeed

Lavender...
I am enchanted by His loveliness,
how enticing is His charm

Blue...
He makes my impossible possible,
He is my life source

Rose bud...
A demonstration of His glory, open
to reveal a sincere fragrance

Leaves of the Rose...
A symbolic expression of my hope in Him

In the garden of my heart, I plant all kinds of roses
A variety of colours
The creative spirit of love.

'The Lord God planted a garden eastward in Eden and there He put the man whom He had formed.
Genesis 2:8 KJV

Here I go again…Reflecting!

ARE YOU?

Asking Abba to search my life
I am always looking for ways to improve
me, keen to find things
I may have missed.

Living at my optimal best
is important to me.
The Lord God of heaven knows
me better than me that is why
He is my internal coach.

SEARCH MY LIFE

Search my life, Oh Lord
As only You can
Let Your all-seeing eyes
navigate the internal me
Resurrect my soul that it may magnify You.
Oh, that my soul will praise You
As I kneel before You Oh Lord,
Search the corners of my mind
Lord purify my heart, cleanse it from hidden sins
Increase my spiritual discernment
Reveal to me the sins that blind my eyes
Draw my attention to things that
so easily befall me.
So, as I kneel before You now
I can intercede and make things right.
O! That I will dismiss my flesh and
walk by Your spirit
Then truly I am released in truth, to worship You.

O LORD, You have searched me
And You know me.
Psalm 139: 1KJV

Come on...

Let me take you down the road of wisdom and show you a child's heart.

The Lord God Almighty, He is not only a God of love, He is also a God of Justice, capable of extreme wrath, but incredibly, at least I believe that, He has a great sense of humour. If you take the time to get to know Him He will set your mind ablaze with laughter. Sometimes as I am contemplating His love, I consider Psalm 8:4, where an angel asked Him,

Lord, what are human beings that You care for them, mere mortals that You think of them? Psalm 144:3 NIV

I imagine the angel was perplexed with God's patience for mankind. I get a picture of him quizzing God...

Why are You, the ultimate Power, putting up with their constant disobedience?

What is so special about this dirt man?

Why are You so compassionate about them? You are always protecting these people! Why?

The angel was confused at how God talks to us, smiles with us, laughs with us. He collects our tears, He grieves, feels our hurts and pains and believe it or not, He is playful, with an appetite for fun.

The God that I serve, He really enjoys the innocence of children.

But Jesus said, "Let the children come to me. Don't stop them! For the Kingdom of Heaven belongs to those who are like these children." Matthew 19:15 NLT

Before you read the next poem, do yourself a favour - drop your guard, let go of your highfaluting principles and become a child before the King... Don't take yourself so seriously ...SMILE!
You really need to read this poem with the heart and voice of a child...

At this stage of our journey we are going to play PEEK-A-BOO!

PEEK-A-BOO

Peek-a-boo
Round and round the throne room
My Lover, Where are Youu?
I seek Youu
Search till I find Youu
Finding You while You may be found.

Peek-a-boo
Where are Youu?
One...two...three...four...
Coming to get Youu
I know You can see me
I know You can hear me
I now You're not far
Peek-a-boo
Where are Youu?
Round and round Your kingdom
Through all the treasures in the house
Ummm lots of goodies... *so that's where You hide them!*

Peek-a-boo
Where are Youu?
Ready or not I'm coming
Still searching for Youu
Coming to Your prayer chamber
BOO......Got You
Knew You were never far.

Lo, children are an heritage of the Lord: and
the fruit of the womb is His reward.
Psalms 12: 3 KJV

More Child-like Passion...

I have worked in the field of counselling and play specialism for many years, in all kinds of settings - hospitals, primary and secondary schools, various charities, agencies and organisations, to today - a private and freelance practitioner. My work has introduced me to all calibre of people; families, children and young people, married couples etc. In my now experience I can honestly say, apart from predators of abuse, there is very little that I have not encountered in the counselling room. Admittedly, occasionally someone discloses something that momentarily dazes me, but I am now at the stage in my professional development where very little phases me. Needless to say, with all my expertise in my field, I am mused working therapeutically with young children. I know so many therapists, who, just the thought of working with a four-year-old made them cringe...but I find children fascinating. If they have a voice, they just say it like it is, without filter. They ask the most embarrassing questions and do the most extraordinary things. Unlike adults, children operate in an authentic realm, very little is hidden and in the therapy room they soon discover the challenging voice called feelings exposure...*I'M SMILING!*

I hear Paul when he says in 1Corinthains 13:11. *When I was a child I talked like a child, I thought like a child, I reasoned like a child. When I became a man I did away with childish things (AMP)* I hear that quite clearly and I completely agree that we should all mature with age...HOWEVER! Let me remind you about what Jesus said when His disciples tried to shoo the children away from Him...

When Jesus saw what was happening He was angry with His disciples. He said to them "Let the children come to me. Don't stop them! For the Kingdom of God belongs to those who are like these children." Mark 10:14...And there are so many more verses of scripture where references are made regarding children, the significance of their childlike mannerism and how they are perceived by God.

I say all the above to say this: in all my growth and development, I still have an area of childlikeness within me. I have a vivid imagination and my creativity is mainly around the heart of a child. Many times I go to God like a child. I often see myself in God's throne room at His feet painting His toenails and practicing nail art. Like a child, I sometimes vision myself giving Him lots of lipstick kisses. I often see Him raising His eyebrow because Esha is walking down the aisle to His throne. In my bedroom I have even danced with the Holy Spirt. I am unashamedly unapologetic about my childish behaviour with my daddy King!

MY ABBA

Good night Abba
Look after me while I sleep
Look after my family, and friends
Sweet dreams to You too.
Kiss, kiss good night

Hello Abba I'm up
Are You up?
I'm not being cheeky
I know You never sleep...just checking!

Abba, what did You do last night while I was sleeping?
You sent me a dream! **You did!**
A nice one, just like I asked for! **You did!**
Don't remember it, I slept so sound

Abba what else did You do?
Looked after me like I asked!
Kept me alive...**WOW**
You sent me a big angel
He stood by my bed all night...**WOW**

Abba what did else did the angel do?
He covered me with hand prints of blood!
Why did he do that Abba, **why?**
When death walked past and saw the blood
he knew not this soul tonight...**WOW, WOW, WOW**

ABBA CAN I GIVE YOU A HUG?
THANK YOU FOR LOVING ME SO

WOW!

The Lord shall preserve you from all evil:
He shall preserve your soul.
Psalms 12:7 KJV

I watched the Passion of Christ once and ONE TIME was enough. It may have been okay for you, but for me, I was horrified. I gritted my teeth, I clenched my toes inside my shoes. The truth is, I couldn't even pretend to be brave, I was quivering inside and bawling on the outside...Boo woo woo...I did not care who could hear. I am not ashamed to say I cried in the packed cinema. It was tortuous, the brutality of the beating was too much. I remember arriving at the cinema and to my amazement the audience were predominately Muslims, and at the start they made the most noise, but when the film ended, you could hear a pin drop; Total Hush. Such was the impact. Everyone, of every race, of whatever faith, walked out in silence. The Passion of the Christ melted the hearts of everyone present. Every time the thought crosses my mind, I think, Lord, You love me so much!
Let me remind you again, if you were the only soul (person) on this earth worth saving, Christ would still have gone to the cross and died!

Who does that?

Yeshua!

Doesn't it just blow your mind?

It is the purest form of LOVE
No earthly person can offer you that kind of LOVE
only God the Father
He is LOVE and His LOVE is perfect!
On the cross Christ exclaimed
Forgive them Lord they know not what they do!
He also proclaimed
IT IS FINISHED
That's LOVE!

FOR ME

My Lover, He loves me with an everlasting love
Teardrops of blood He cried
For me
Stripped of His garments and humiliated
For me
A crown of thorns He wore
For me
A slaughterous beating He took
For me
Brutally hammered to a tree
For me
For hours He hung in thirst
For me
A sword thrust in His side
For me
Yes, He bled and died
For me
My Lover, He loves me with an everlasting love
He went to hell and back
For me.

Who gave Himself a ransom
for all, to be testified in due time.
1 Timothy 2:6 KJV

MY LOVER HAS BLOOD STAINED HANDS.

Excuse me!

Have you seen my Lover?
He has no comeliness that you should desire Him
But have you seen Him?
He has blood stained hands
Look in His face
His forehead has the piercing of thorns

Excuse me!

Have you seen my Lover?
He's not beautiful
His appearance may make you turn away
His back has been gauged with a whip
His flesh may be hanging from His body
If you look closely
You'll see He has been savagely beaten

Excuse me!

Have you seen my Lover?
They call Him King of the Jews
His feet have nail prints in them
Look into His eyes
They are heavy with tear drops of blood
Reach up and kiss His lips
They are sodden with vinegar

Excuse me!

Have you seen my Lover?
They call Him a trouble maker
Look at His face
His cheeks are polluted with spit

His side has a hole from the stabbing
of a sword
He is half naked
His clothes were rented from Him

Excuse me!

Have you seen my Lover?
You can't miss Him
He has blood stained hands
His back is laden with stripes
Thirty-eight and one for me.
They wrapped death cloth around Him
They locked Him out of sight.

Excuse me!

Have you seen my Lover?
I'm looking for Him because I need him
It's okay! I see Him
I see my Lover.
There He is; I see Him.
I see Him, sitting on the right hand
side of my King.
Making intercession for me.

But He was wounded for our transgression,
He was bruised for our iniquities;
the chastisement of our peace was upon Him;
and with His stripes we are healed.
Isaiah 53:5 KJV

BLOOD DROPS

My stomach churns with sadness
To see the world push away those blood-stained hands
The offer available to heal mankind...turned away
Open compassion, mocked and jeered
Yeshua the reconciler still persecuted today
Makes me sad!

He is the Passover Lamb
Yet the world...it passes over Him
He was crucified to save the world
Yet... daily they choose to crucify Him afresh
No remorse...no guilt...no shame...no care
Most believe faith in Him has long gone dim
For them the light went out when man stepped in
I'm okay being anchored in Him.

A life-giving spirit refused by a decaying world
Deceived by the victory of human knowledge
Ever learning but never coming
to the fullness of truth
The essence of pure undiluted love...
extensive divinity
Ears open but never hearing the gentle
sounds of the Holy Spirit
CALLING
Bright eyes without true vision...
unable to see the signs of the times
Minds closed to the POWER that can enable them
to live in peace in these times of uncertainties
The Resurrected Saviour, Reconciler,
The Way, The Truth, The Life

R...E...J...E...C...T...E...D

The world choosing to sit for a season in darkness
They've missed His tears!
Blood Drops!
Died that not one soul would be lost!
And being in agony, He prayed more earnestly. Then His sweat became like great drops of blood falling down to the ground.
Luke 22:44 KJV

Isaiah 52: 14

But as many looked in wonder when they saw Him.
His face was disfigured He seemed hardly human,
and from His appearance, one would scarcely
know He was a man. NLT

Please take the time to read and
re-read the above verse.
I want you to really get a vivid picture that
Christ Jesus was brutally, savagely, horrifically,
mercilessly, beaten beyond recognition.

The film the Passion of the Christ was
a true depiction
of the horror of the cross.
All for you. All for me. All for mankind
He is my miracle. He SUFFERED, He SUFFERED,
He S-U-F-F-E-R-E-D and died for me.
So leave me alone to serve my King
He deserves all of my praise!

GLOOOOORRRY!

For God so loved the world that He gave His one and only Son, that whoever believes in Him should not perish, but have eternal life.
John 3:16 KJV

ROYAL BLOOD OF ETERNAL LIFE

A hammer with penetrating force
Sharpened nails held by human hands
A rugged tree, there He hung
Exposed; He was a mark of shame
Yet, little was it known
Today, my Lover's BLOOD still stands
The expansion of dripping hands splattered soo wide
Can't get around it
Elevated; reaches soo high
Can't get over it
Flows in the valley, soo deep
Can't get under it
The Royal Blood of Eternal Life
Can't get around it
Can't get over it
Can't get under it
But, for sure, those loving Blood-Stained Hands
Can take you through it.

Jesus said to Him, "I am the way, and the truth, and the life.
No one comes to the Father except through me.
John 14:6 ESV

Some years ago, I read an article, a true story, about a Christian couple whose daughter was born prematurely and spent the first few months of her life in hospital in an incubator on the neonatal unit. They prayed and visited their daughter every day and eventually their baby was well enough to go home.

About five years later, the little girl was walking in the park with her mother (if I can remember the story correctly). As she neared a lake in the park she began to sniff and smell the air. As she sniffed, her mother became a little curious and asked what she was doing. The little girl looked at her mother and smiled, "I'm smelling" she said. Her mother replied, "I think you can smell the rain coming." The little girl continued sniffing, turning to her mum she said, "No, it's not the rain, it smells like Him." Her mother looked at her a little puzzled. She enquired, "What do you mean?" The little girl continued, "It smells like Him, the one who came to see me when I was in the hospital, He came and talked to me when you weren't there. It smells like Him." It didn't take long for the little girl's mother to realised her daughter was talking about Jesus. She also had some information she could not have known because she was a baby. Her mother was flabbergasted by what her daughter had said. Jesus was the answer to their prayer. He was there with them in their times of despair He saved their daughter's life.

When the Holy Spirit reminded me about this article, I had to share it.
I am curled up on my settee right now deep in contemplation...
I am thinking, "What does the Lord smell like?

The truth is, most young children are so blatantly honest! Jesus has a scent, I know, because this story was a genuine account about His smell and it must be a sweet- smelling savour because children are not good with keeping their mouths shut. They will tell you if someone or something smells rancid...

What are your thoughts about the atmosphere and the scent of God?

The Fragrance of the King!

I think Lord that You smell like Roses
You are the Rose of Shar'on
I think Lord You smell like Lilies
You are the Lily of the Valley
Then again Lord You may smell like...
The healing balm of Frankincense
Or even the holy oil of Myrrh
Or even the delicate essence of olive oil.

I think Lord that You smell like...
Freshly baked bread from the oven
For You are the bread of life
I think Lord You smell like...
Sacramental wine made from the finest grapes
Your Blood was shed to save us.

I think possibly Lord, You smell like
The anointing oil of Spikenard,
That moisturised Your body in preparation
for Your death
Or even like the treasure of Aloe Vera,
The spices of Saffron, Calamus and Cinnamon
That embalmed Your broken and battered
body for burial

I think Lord You smell like...
The garden dew on resurrection morning
That freshened the atmosphere of reconciliation
I think most of all Lord You smell like...
A sacrificial aroma of Love
The incense of peace, joy and the hope of salvation.

Certainly Lord, You smell like the gift
of everlasting life

Then the Lord said to Moses
"Gather fragrant spices – resin droplets, mollusk shell
And galbanum – and mix these fragrant spices with pure frankincense.
Weight out in equal amounts.

Using the usual techniques of the incense maker, blend the spices together and sprinkle them with salt to produce a pure and holy incense. Grind some of the powder and put it in front of the Ark of the Covenant, where I will meet with you in the Tabernacle. You must treat this incense as Most Holy.
Exodus 30:34-36

I read the next poem at a seminar, 2007, and during my reading the workshop facilitator, who had flown in from South Africa, got up and began to dance to the words. I was amazed! I had never seen anyone do creative dance to poetry before. I think she astonished everyone. Later that afternoon she photocopied the poem and got everyone into groups of threes. She gave each group three lines each from the poem and gave them about twenty minutes to come up with a creative dance. It was absolutely incredible. The young people came up with their street dances, some did flowing actions, some did various forms of praise dances with ballet movements; even the men danced. That day I learnt something new about poetry. It was then I realised that our God is a God of creativity in every aspect of life. After-all, in six days, He created the heavens and the earth, the sun, the moon, the birds of the air, the animals, the trees and herbs; and from the dust of the ground He formed man. And get this - from a rib taken from the side of the man, He created the woman, IN STYLE...NOW! That is creativity.

Whether you sing, dance, write songs, script writer, poet, artist, musician, fashion designer, teacher or gardener - you could be a mechanic, engineer, doctor, shop assistant, chef, hairdresser, work in the beauty industry, inventor, TV personality, or play sports. You could simply be a great parent or carer and I could go on and on. Whatever talent or creative skills God has given to you, whether big or small, DO NOT! And I quote again, DO NOT, allow anyone to stifle your gift. You have a responsibility to shine your light in this world. Your gift is God's investment in you

The heavens declare the glory of God; and the
firmament shows His handy work.
Psalm 19:1 KJV

POWER OF LOVE

The Power of Love
Two hearts entwined
Passion engrossed... Soul tie
Who can separate me from my Lover's grasp?
Am I not infatuated by **HIM**?
Is HE not awesome?

Spirit to spirit connection
Who can thrust me from **HIS** arms?
Who can untangle our hearts?
Who can entice me from **HIS** love?
Hear me when I say!
NOTHING... NOTHING & NOTHING
Can separate me from **MY KING**
I am one hundred percent certain
Without a shadow of doubt, **THAT...**
Not family, not children, not friends, not employment
Not tribulation, or persecution, distress or bomb
Not north, south, east or west
Not height, width or depth

I am assured **THAT...**
Not mockery, laughter, ridicule, media
Past history, present situation, things to come
Life, death or anything else...

Can loosen the truth of love entwined...
I am saturated i**n HIM.**

Together my **Lover My King & I**
Are-- more --than –conquerors!

NOBODY! Can separate me from the **POWER of HIS LOVE.**

For I am persuaded, that neither death, nor life, nor angels, nor principalities, nor things present, nor things to come, nor height, nor depth, nor any other creature, shall be able to separate us from the love of God, which is in Christ Jesus. Romans 8:38-39.

Have you ever knelt down to pray and you are suddenly lost for words? You are completely dumb-struck. You kneel for what seems like an eternity, unable to make a sound. You have so much in your heart but nothing comes from your lips. Tears are rolling down your face, and you find yourself flat on the floor. All you can do is lie, kneel or sit there and wait; you want to speak but you can't. You just feel helpless under the power and anointing of the Holy Spirit? I say no more...

SILENTLY WAITING

I lay prostrate across the floor
In reverence I bring myself to you
Words, they fail me I cannot speak
Utter I try, but only a sullen sound.

From the depth of my bowels I'm groaning
Yet only my silence is known
I feel the gentle breeze of Your breath
The touch of Your presence around me
An attempt I make not, to speak,
My words I know, they fail me.
The warmth of Holiness flowing through my veins
All the cells in my being are shedding tears

Paralyse, I cannot... unable... to move
Your love, Your passion for me so strong

Crippled before Your throne I am.
Words, disappeared, completely gone
So, I must continue to lie prostrate
Silently across the floor and wait.

That the Lord direct your heart into the love of God,
and into the patient waiting for Christ.
2 Thessalonians 3: 5 KJV

THE SILENCE OF MY LOVER'S HEART

The silence of Your heart, my Love
rings louder in my ears than spoken words
amplified by the loudest speakers.
Attentively I am listening
to hear Your quiet loud sound.

In my stillness I hear the whisper of Your heartbeat
I listen to Your musical sound
The gentle rhythmic loudness.
Only I can hear the music, for You have my heart
Only I can feel that loud silent beat
Only I can feel Your touch opening a pathway
the length and breadth of my mind.

I feel the warmth of our penetrating eyes
Searching the depth of my being
I can taste the affection of Your love
Let me savour every moment of our oneness
I welcome the gentle sound of Your Spirit
I hear its loud silence calling.

I hear volume of Your sound...It's Silent!
Only I can feel the breeze of Your breath
Breathing wholeness into my soul.
Yes! The silence of Your Heart, my Love
Speaks louder than spoken words.

When You said, "Seek My face"
My heart said to You, "Your face, Lord I will seek.
Psalm 27:8 NKJV

As I have become more intimate with God, I have found that in prayer, I don't need to shout. God is not deaf, so sometimes there is no need for the...**AND LORRD...JESUSSS, WE'RE ASKING YOU TO HAVE MERCY...AND YES LORRD, WE KNOW THAT YOU ARE THE HEALERRR...AND LORRD, AS WE COME BEFORE YOUU... LORRDD....**

Time and place for everything, sometimes the loudness is irrelevant, some of us Christians need to calm down; most of the bawling out and shouting in prayer is often just habitual amongst some Christians. There is nowhere in the scriptures where it tells us that Jesus shouted His prayer at the top of His voice or that God is audible-impaired. God also hear our prayers in quietness. If you don't believe, read 1Samuel 1:1-15.

I may not be a fervent prayer warrior but I have learnt to pray. You do not need a university degree, you do not need to be a theologian, you do not need pastoral position and there is certainly no need for the shouting sometimes...you don't need to bawl the Lord out of heaven. He is omnipresent. The Holy Spirit is right beside you. You do not need the... **LORRRRD...** All you need is a relationship with Jesus and heart and mind to hear and receive from Him.

QUIET TIMES

It's in those quiet times
That You reveal Your heart to me

It's in those quiet times
That You let me know who You are
It's in those quiet times
That You tell me how much You love me
It's in those quiet times
That You cause me to see Your overflow

It's in those quiet times
That our hearts connect

It's in those quiet times
That I can hear Your heart beat

It's in those quiet times
That You search my soul

It's in those quiet times
That we truly embrace.

And after the earthquake a fire; but the Lord was not in the fire:
and after the fire a still small voice.
1 Kings 19:12 KJV

Some years ago, 2004, I enrolled at the School of Psalmody; A Worship Lifestyle for people who know their God. The course was founded in 1983, by Tom Inglis from New Zealand. His purpose is to help God's people to develop a lifestyle of worship in their lives, their homes and local churches. The aim and objectives are that the body of Christ would become effective witnesses in their community and worldwide. Over thirteen weeks the course covered many aspects of worship including: Worship lifestyle, worship & thanksgiving, worship & warfare, healing & worship, the Holy Spirit & worship, Glory & worship, Giving & worship and much more.
My life has not been the same since. I have learnt to give God praise regardless of how I am feeling. I cannot expect anything from God if I am not prepared to give Him what belongs to Him. I was created to worship Him. I have discovered and proven that when my praises go up my blessing come down. I actually find it very difficult to not lift my hands during a worship service. He deserves the glory.

In his book, *The Purpose and Power of Praise and Worship,* Myles Munroe wrote:

Praise is seeking God
Worship is being found by Him.

My interpretation of this is, Praise is calling God. If I want God's attention, I need to lift my hands, open my mouth in loud praise to honour Him. Worship is listening to God. If I want to hear from Him, I need to bow down in worship and quiet my soul before Him.

What is your understanding of praise and worship?

There are occasions during the day when I simply stop what I am doing and lift my hands in appreciation to God. Yes, I do agree we need to know the word of God, but our main focus, I believe, is to praise and worship Him. Our daily lifestyle should be a reflection of who He is.

The next poem is about my favourite part of the course, the Seven Hebrew words for praise. If you take the time to study them, they will transform your relationship with the King of kings.

PRAISE HIM

Give Him adoration
Confess; open your soul before Him
Let the rivers of life pour from you
Let out a sacrifice of praise
TOWDAH HIM!

Throw your hands towards heaven
Appreciate Him with extended arms
Lavish Him with thanksgiving
Remember the Lord God your CREATOR
Lift up His Name on high
YADAH HIM!

Shout to the Lord
Let loose, run around, get crazy
Give inhibited triumphant praise
Shout the praise of deliverance
Let the voice of His people be heard
SHABACH HIM!

Sing; make melody with your voice
Pluck the stringed instruments
Beat the drums, shake the tambourines
Blow the shofar
Let music ring in His ears
ZAMAR HIM!

Make a boast in Him
Become clamorously foolish for Him
Celebrate in crazy rage praise

Honour His glory
Praise Him with every breath of life
HALAL HIM!

Put on your garment of praise
Stand in righteousness before Him
Give to Him a life style of holiness
Worship Him from the beauty of your inner man
Let your spirit enthrone Him
Magnify the inhabitation of His truth
TEHILLAH HIM!

Kneel before Him
Revere and adore Him
Rest in His presence
Mediate upon His goodness
Prepare your heart to receive from Him
Bless Him for who He is.
BARAK HIM!

Praise Him for His mighty acts:
Praise Him according to His excellent greatness.
Psalm 15:2 KJV

You will find through this journey, I use the word 'transform' many times. That is because I really want mind change. I don't want ordinary, I want unique. Of all the things on earth God is most proud of, it's me. He is most of proud of you.

Who takes time to number the hairs
on someone's head?
God does!
Just imagine He knows the follicles on a bald head.

Who takes time to monitor your thoughts?
God does.
Who takes time to read and listen to your heart?
God does.

Who takes time to fully invest in you even when you
feel your gift is not big enough to make a significant
contribution to the world?
God does.

Who knows you better than you?
God does.

Who believes in you and knows that you can?
God does

Who defines and qualifies you for greatness?
God does.

Isn't that cause to worship Him?

**It's cause enough for me to always be asking Him
to draw out the worshipper in me.**

The next poem was written on one of my low days when I had to spend some time encouraging myself...God knows!

Worshipper in Me

Spirit of the living God fall afresh upon me.
Draw the worshipper out of me
Holy Spirit transform my mind; change my heart
Mould me and make into Your honoured vessel.

Lord anoint me, release me
Let the flesh in me die so the
worshipper in me can take its place
Let the worshipper in me present
itself in the fullness of joy
Lord, let the loudness of the praise
inside of me flow out my mouth
So that my voice of thanksgiving can
be heard in heaven's ears.

Lord, hear my struggles today
My heart longs for You
Touch the deepness in me with Your refreshing oil
Let the worshipper in me be heard among
all the hosts of heaven.
Lord, I need Your help to release my voice of silence
Let me hear Your Holy Spirit dancing
inside me once again
Hear my plea, stir the praise within me.
Let the worshipper in me come forth
to pronounce a blessing to You
My Lord, my God, my King, the strength
of my life
I hunger for You
Help me close the distance that I have
created between You and me!

Invest in me once again; release the adoration in me
Cause the worshipper in me to flame
like fire and magnify You
and bless Your Name in all truth.

I love the Lord, for he heard my voice: he heard my cry for mercy.
Because He turned His ear to me. I will call on Him as long as I live
Psalm 116:2 NIV

Can I be truthful? Is that okay?

As I have matured in my walk of faith, I have learnt that even the most seasoned Christians, for reasons unknown, have a down day. The Psalms evidently describes King David, as zealous as he was for God, as having many down days. He was a man after God's heart but it didn't stop him from sometimes feeling down in the dumps and anxious about life. I occasionally have those days and it is at those times, when I begin my day in my emotions, that I turn to the Holy Spirit to help me take control of my flesh. I just need Him to help me change my mind-set before toxicity sets in. That is when I give Him permission to help me rise above my feelings and focus on my present, instead of re-living the traumas of my past.

The next poem is about where my mind can take and has taken me...but for the mercy and grace of God.

WHEN I NEED YOU MOST!

When self-judgement renders me powerless
Lord, that's when I need You most
When my mind is fierce in contempt against me
That's when I need to hear You say, peace be still.
When my lack of wisdom causes me to resurrect
a thought from the sea of forgetfulness
When the mess of my past smirks at me,
filling my heart with sorrow
When I malfunction in feelings of regrets and underserved love
That's when I need Your splattered blood of comfort
For it will render me free and give me peace that
surpasses all understanding.

When my doubts point me backwards
That's when I need You to secure my life upon
Your solid foundation
For only You my Lord can untangle me from the
fireworks of my past shooting at me.
I place my head in Your bosom to hear
Your quiet whisper
soothing my mind of despair
Only for a moment
For I know You will keep me.

When my distress seems great
And my Jericho wall is fast erecting
Past pains, hurts, try to keep me hostage
and shut You out
Lord, that's when I need You most
To dismiss the diabolical thoughts trying
to lock the door

For I need You to come in and eat with me
And feed me with Your word of life.

When my body tries to force me to look back
And try to cement me like a pillar of salt
That's when I need You most Lord
To refocus my carnal mind from overflowing flesh.
When I recall my ways that were not pleasing to You
That's when I need You most
To bleach me with the truth
For You no longer remember my sins.

When I make attempts to untie forgotten baggage
Lord, that's when I need You most
To give me wisdom to execute good self-judgement
For You see me with a heart of forgiveness.
When my flesh tries to blackmail me with unbelief
That's when I need You Lord
To set up a standard against the spirit of doubt

When confusion tries to strangle me
That's when I need You most Lord
To bring my mind under the subjection
of Your Holy Spirit
And remind me that You are not the
author of confusion.
When anxiety makes me tremble and shake
That's when I need You most Lord
To lead me beside calm waters to still my soul
For in Your arms of compassion I need
not be anxious for nothing.
Let me bask in the presence of Your Holiness
For in Your presence Lord, there is fullness of joy.

When my past steps in my way and blurs my vision
That's when I need You most Lord
To give me spiritual eyes to see my way on
the narrow pathway of grace.
When strongholds try to capture me
again and catapult bricks of fear at me
That's when I need You most Lord
To draw Your sword to protect my mind
For You have not given me a spirit of fear
But of power, love and a sound mind.

When my heart is overwhelmed
Lord, that's when I need You most
To rescue me from the torment of me
The negative me voice, spitting accusations,
trying to shame me
That's when I need You most Lord
To help me separate from self-sabotage
Mostly I need You Lord
To help me put down the internal boxing gloves
That has battered my heart and still trying to punch my mind
For my past is over
I AM RESTORED...NO LONGER BOUND!
I HAVE BEEN SET FREE
And Who the SON has set Free is Free Indeed!

*"For I know the thoughts that
I think towards you, say the LORD, thoughts of peace
and not of evil, to give you a future and a hope."
Jeremiah 29:11*

CALL HIM....
YESHUA...YESHUA...YESHUA
JESUS...JESUS...JESUS
MESSIAH...MESSIAH...MESSIAH

WONDERFUL
COUNSELLOR
MIGHTY GOD
EVERLASTING FATHER
PRINCE OF PEACE

I am reading Philippians chapter 2, reflecting in awe at the Lover of my soul. Verses 7-8, the writer reminds us that Jesus chose to give up all His divine heavenly privileges, humbled Himself, took on human form to come to earth, took on all our sins, and died like a common criminal on the cross so that you and I could reconcile and be in relationship with our Creator. How Great is our God!

Verses 9-11 tell us that our Saviour is elevated to the highest place of honour. He has a name above all names and at the name of 'JESUS' every knee should bow in heaven and earth and under the earth and every tongue declare that Jesus Christ is Lord... Glory to our Father in heaven...

Don't know about you, but for sure, when my heart is overwhelmed, I can call the ROCK who is higher than I.

This morning...

I was sitting on my settee in full thought, reminiscing on the past. I suppose I was feeling a little disappointed with myself for spending so much of my life getting it wrong, for not realising who Christ really was and is. It was like I was kicking myself for my ignorance of missing what was in plain sight... the splendour of the King...He is so patient and long-suffering. All these years He has being waiting for me to take my eyes off man and fix them on Him. He has been waiting for me to stop fighting about what was out of my control and focus on what I can control, and that is working out my own salvation with Him.

Now that He has my full attention...like the song...I just keep falling in love with Him over and over again.

SO IN LOVE WITH YOU

The more I think about You
The more I fall in love with You
I no longer want to know about You
I want to know You
I set my sight upon You
For there is no other God like You.
Lord! Who is like unto You?
Surely, You are the Lord my strength
Deliberately, I create passion in my soul for You
Sometimes I just break in Your presence
Teardrops from my heart to YOU...sealed with a kiss.
To know You My King is to truly exist
I am so in love with You!
Lord I love You soooooo much
Sorry it's taken so long to realise
Lover of my soul
I love You sooo much
.......Words can't...they just CAN'T......

How precious are Your thoughts about me, O God.
They cannot be numbered!
Psalm 139:17

AGAPE!

Agape is the Greek word for LOVE. Amazingly, in my research, I discovered Love Styles by John Lee 1993. His theory is that there are several kinds of love. When it came to Agape, he wrote and I quote:

"Agapic love is self-sacrificing all compassing love. Agapic lovers are often spiritual or religious people. Agapic lovers view their partners as blessings and take care of them. Agapic lovers remain faithful to their partners to avoid causing them pain. Often they wait patiently for their partners after a break up. Marriage and children are sacred. Trust and sex is a gift between two people. Agapic love is unconditional."

I have discovered other meanings for the usage of the word agape but the one that interests me most is the Greek meaning: God is Love as opposed to mere human love.

Theos en agape....God is love
Love (agapao) the Lord with all your heart and with all your soul and with all your mind.
Love (agapao) your neighbour as yourself.

One other thing John Lee said about the Agapic Lover is that they are capable of being taken advantage of, occasionally they feel used. I use this sentence to illustrate that God's love is pure with no alternate motives. However, God's people are sometimes guilty of taking advantage of His Son when they cannot fully commit to Him. They walk back and forth, falling in and out of love with Him and some even walk away from Him, forgetting all He has done for them, having to run back to Him in repentance, crucifying Him all over again, putting Him to an open shame. *(Hebrews 6:1-6)*

My God, My KING where would I be without
Your heart of forgiveness?

Like King David, often I sit in reflection and considered...

"Where would I be Lord, if You were not on my side?"

Yeshua, my Love, where would I be without
Your sacrificial love?

Holy Spirit, where would I be if I could not rest in
Your loving comfort?

My King, God Most High, "Where would I be without
Your guidance and protection?"

AGAPE

The purest Love
Unblemished Love...
Not sensual......Clean Love
Agape.......Unconditional
Morally beautiful
Sacrificial.........Agape
Truly immeasurable
Agape.........Divine
Outstandingly impeccable
Perfect.......Agape.

Pure, merciful, compassionate, selfless, unfailing, charitable, kind, hopeful, truthful, long suffering, patient, joyful, friendship, full of glory.

Lord You are simply Amazing!

All of me LOVES All of You!
In this moment everything in me is giving You Praise

Thank You for loving Me!

Thank You for looking beyond all my faults
and meeting me at my place of need.

Beloved, let us love one another: for love is of God; and every one that loves is born of God, and knows God.
1 John 4: 7 KJV

Real love is when lovers' hearts cannot bear to be apart. My Lover, cannot bear to be separated from me. We are in constant communication in prayer, thought, heart and mind; totally roped in spirit Right now, He is at the right hand of His Father interceding on my behalf. His hands are lifted in agreement for me. His Love is tireless. He puts in great effort to keep me mentally sound. He is fully alert to my emotional frequency, His heavenly transmitters are always prepared for my call. His love for me in everlasting. When I say I adore my maker, make no mistake that every inch of my seen outside dirt merged with all my internal organs, unseen spirit and everything else that I am, are inseparably fixated on Him!

As I said before, and I know for sure about My Lover, if I was the only one on earth worth dying for, He still would have died. How comforting is my hope in Him.

That's called REAL Love!
It just brings Tears to my Heart.

Does your heart sometimes cry for Him?

TEARS IN MY HEART

I kneel before You Lord
Tears in my heart
I come to bow my soul down to You
My heart is breaking in two
With the love I have for You.
Nothing can separate me from You Lord
Nothing can ever stop me serving You
'Cause You are my light and my salvation,
My joy, who keeps me in perfect peace
You are my friend, my banner and victory.

I kneel before You Lord
Tears in my heart
I come to bow myself down to You
My heart is breaking in two
With the love I have for You.

Wrap Your strong arms around me
Like the eagle protects her chick
Over-shadow me with Your glory
Let me feel Your presence
Heartbeat to heartbeat connection
I kneel in awe of You.

I kneel before You Lord
Tears in my heart
I come to bow down and worship You
My heart is breaking in two
With the love I have for You.

The way I feel about You
Words can hardly express
My mind, my thoughts, all in me
Entangled with Your awesomeness.

For the Lamb which is in the midst of the throne shall feed them,
and shall lead them unto living fountains of waters: and
God shall wipe away all tears from their eyes.
Revelations 7:17 KJV

Touch not God's anointed. (1Chronicles 16:22)

This verse in the bible has been so misrepresented, misused and manipulated. In my ignorant church days, I heard many leaders own this scripture as though it was especially reserved for them. They made reference to this scripture as though it was their personal entitlement. It is such a tragedy when men and women of God, *who began their ministry in the pureness of faith,* reach a self-gratifying stage, believing they are above everyone else.

....GET REAL...I am God's anointed too.

"Touch not mine anointed and do my prophets no harm.
Psalm105:15

King David wrote this Psalm in reference to the Ark of the Covenant. He was giving God thanks when it was returned to Israel. What was King David actually saying when he wrote this? I believe, in my opinion, David was saying this...

We are God's chosen people and His prophets are His voice here on earth, Touch Us Not. David was proclaiming that Israel was under the protection of the Most High God, so be careful. He was saying, look, many kings and nations have already been destroyed for Israel's sake, so leave us alone because it is too high a price to pay. He was saying, be very clear, we are a chosen people, a special possession. Our invisible God, the God of heaven's armies, is ready to do battle for us... So Enemy Go Away!

David did not refer to himself, singularly, he referred to the children of Israel, plural. However, under the new covenant, anyone who confesses that Jesus Christ is Lord, that He is risen from the dead and has ascended to His Father in heaven, anyone who believes He is coming back again, anyone who is protected and is covered by His blood, anyone who does His will, anyone whose final destination is in the heavenly kingdom of El Shaddai, the Almighty God, *IS ANOINTED.*

When God says touch not my anointed, He means do not interfere with my people, they are my bride, if you put your hand on them, I am going to deal with your case.

Let me conclude by telling you this: if you are a child of the King, serving Him whole-heartedly, giving Him your best, then you are ......

CALLED, CHOSEN, ANOINTED AND APPOINTED FOR HIS PURPOSE!

TOUCH NOT

Touch not
I am joint heir to His throne
Touch me not
I am called by Him
Touch not
I have been chosen by Him
Touch me not
I am anointed by Him
Touch not
I am appointed by Him
Touch me not
God of heaven's armies
My Lover, He is armed and dangerous

Touch Me Not.

Moreover whom He predestined, these He also called,
Whom He called, these He also justified:and
whom He justified, them He also glorified.
Romans 8:30 KJV

JEALOUS LOVER

The Love of my life is a Jealous Lover
From before the foundation of the world
He has loved me.
Before I was conceived in my mother's womb
He knew me
Like a faithful Shepherd He has fed me
From the greenest pastures
Like a Hawk He carefully watches over me
He is a Jealous Lover
Like a Golden Eagle He commands
His authority for me
He is a Jealous Lover
Like a roaring Lion He stands as King in my life
He is a Jealous Lover
Like a gentle Dove He wraps His love around me
He is a Jealous Lover
Like a new born Lamb He gave His life to set me free
He is a Jealous Lover
Prepared to share me with no other
Vengeance upon the thief who steals after me
His wrath will He not spare the deceiver.
He is a Jealous Lover
I am the **APPLE** of His eye.

'For the LORD thy God is a consuming fire, even a Jealous God.'
Deuteronomy 4:24, KJV

I JUST NEED TO GIVE MY KING SOME PRAISE!

HALLELUYAH
HALLELUYAH
HALLELUYAH
GLORRRY TO YOUR NAME LORD
THANK YOU JESUS
GIVE YOU PRAISE
BLESSED BE YOUR HOLY NAME
BLESSINGS AND HONOUR
GLORY AND POWER TO
THE KING OF KINGS
I LIFT UP YOUR NAME ON HIGH. PLACE YOU
ON THE HIGHEST PLACE
MIGHTY ARE THE WORKS OF YOUR HANDS
YOU ARE WORTHY TO BE PRAISED
HALLELUYAH
HOW GREAT YOU ARE LORD
HOW GREAT YOU ARE!
YOU REIGN VICTORIOUS!

Please realise praise is LOUD!
The SHOUT brought the Jericho wall down!

I make no apology for reiterating how much I love the Lord. He truly is incredible. There is just so much mystery about Him, there is always something new to learn about him. The way He orchestrates my life just blows my mind. I just know when He is at work. My goodness, often times, I just shake my head in awe and say, "Holy Spirit, that was You because I didn't think of that, I achieved it, but it wasn't me."

I sometimes sit and consider: "Why would anyone choose to walk away from Him?" I can understand why people may walk away from a congregation...*Let's be honest; sometimes church folks just get on yuh last nerve.* However, making a commitment to serve Christ and falling out of love with Him after He has blessed you many times over is beyond me!

My God is supreme, no one or nothing else can compare. There is no other truth and He is certainly my truth. You cannot walk away from true relationship with God and stay sane.

HIS NAME IS TRUTH!

My Lover, He is called the truth
He is the way! The only way
Yes! Yes! Yes! Yes! Yes!
YES!
Can't get through without Him
The restorer, reconciliator of life
NO!
No through way! No other way but Him.

He is the bread of life! Break Him.
Go on!
Taste and see that He is good
Is your hunger not satisfied?

He is the fountain of living waters
The well of continual overflow
Try the wine!
Drink and never parch again
Is your thirst not quenched?

Take a moment! Savour the flavours
Bread and wine, a perfect combination
Ummm!
Can't spit Him out...can you?
That's because...My King, He is
THE TRUTH!

Taste and see that the Lord is good: blessed
is the man that trusts in Him
Psalm 34:8 KJV

I Love to Praise My King!

Yes, that's one thing I'm known for, praising my Lord with a loud voice. I don't believe in making the effort to get dressed to go to church and sit down looking like lady muck. Nope! No sir! I have no shame in saying it again, I love to praise my God. I remember someone once telling me that I needed to be quiet in church and the answer I gave her was this:

"Telling me that I cannot praise God is like taking my breath away."

Trust me, she never told me to be quiet again. I don't mix my words with anyone who tries to close me down. I was created to worship my King and I will worship Him anywhere in whatever form, I just love my King, *PERIOD.* Saying all this brings to mind a workshop I attended some years ago, 2007...It was about creative worship dance, using flags and banners.

Before my arrival I wasn't quite sure what to expect, so I went along with an open mind. When I walked through the door I was mesmerised; the room had been transformed into an array of colours, the walls, the chairs were dressed and flowing with beautiful materials. Shades of elegant colours were everywhere. It was a stunningly graceful sight. There were flags and prayer shawls, each one printed with the different names of God. I had no idea that our God had so many names. I was astounded to learn that the Lord our God has over two hundred attributes & characteristics and possibly more. I am still amazed now writing about it. Some of the names and attributes were alien to me. I had never received teaching about this in the church I attended.

What a shame we put such limitation on our King. We really need to take Him out of the souvenir box of our minds and let Him loose... He is MEGA. Honestly, the more my knowledge and understanding increase about my King, is the more I love Him.

I challenge you to draw a little closer to Him, because if you draw close to Him, He will draw close to you and allow you to see, like Moses, a glimpse of His majestic splendour.

Moses responded, "Then show me Your glorious presence." Exodus 33:18 NLT
Draw near to God and He will draw near to you
James 4: 8 NKJV

WOW

W.O.W

Panting in my heart
To behold colours of beauty
Takes my breath away
My eyes centred on rays of sunshine
God's glory to behold.

W.O.W

A truly magnificent sight
The majestic colours of the rainbow
My mind in transformation
The grandeur of His Royal Highness
To be worshipped and adored.

W.O.W

A sight to the seeing eyes
The brilliance of the heavens
An expression of His greatness
A creativity of praise
In banners, flags, & prayer shawls
How wonderfully stately and grand.

W.O.W

My mind in wonderment
Thanksgiving in an exploration of colours
Honouring the King of kings
Colours of the earth
Magnifying the GREAT I AM.

Oh worship the Lord in the beauty of holiness:
fear before Him, all the earth.
Psalm 96:9 KJV

TRULY HE IS WORTHY

The King
His Majesty
Bow before Him
Worship & adore Him
Sing to the King
Let your voice be heard
Open your mouth
Praise Him
The King
His Imperial Majesty
Dance in His presence
Move your feet
Glorify Him
Lift your hands to
The King
Bless His name
Let all your being
Exalt Him

FOR TRULY; HE IS WORTHY.

I will call upon the Lord who is worthy to be praised
2 Samuel 22:4 KJV

The world is ever changing and moving at such an incredible pace. To keep up, modern technology has taken the world by storm. Society has created technological gadgets for everything including the way we communicate with each other. We can have a full-blown conversation without physical contact, appearance, or verbal speech. Humanness is no longer relational. We really don't know each other anymore. It's a world of keyboard and pretence. We have locked each other out of our worlds, *'busy being me.'* No time.

We have so much technology yet such little time to crack a smile, too important being me. We literally have to make appointments to see each other. Gone are the days of contact without invite or fore-warning. It appears that technology has created physical distance between us. I am busy being me and I have a machine for doing you. I give God thanks.

The doorway to the throne room of my King is never blocked. There are no locks to keep me out. The pathway to God's ears is always clear, no matter how many of earth's children are calling at the same time. Our God, Lord and Father, the unchanging ever-present One is available twenty-four seven. Free access directly to my Beloved. Instant communication, NEVER too busy for me or for you. That's our King!

FREE ACCESS

Free access to my King
Phone line never busy
Never switched off
No appointment
No engaged tone
No re-dial

No wrong number
No operator
No answering machine
No message ignored
No waiting in a queue
No music to distract you
No being recorded for training purposes

No identity checking
No getting through to the wrong department
No putting you on hold
No systems failure
No technical interference
No language barrier
No passing you onto someone else.
No making me cuss

No call back tomorrow
No charge! Totally free
Direct access, never denied
Free access to My King!

USERNAME...THE HOLY SPIRIT!
PASSWORD...JESUS!

For He is our peace, who has made one, and has broken down the middle wall of partition between us.
Ephesians 2:14

Time is such a precious gift.

Just to think, the Lord God of heaven, creator of the universe, always, always has time for me and He has time for you. As mortals, our life here on earth is limited. Hebrew 9:27 tells us *"It is appointed unto man once to die and then the judgement."*. Whoever we are, whatever status, age, gender, race, poor or rich, one day our life on earth will end......a subject most like to avoid, but it is inevitable. Whilst we have life we have to respect and honour time. James 4:14 states: *"Yet we do not know what tomorrow will bring. What is your life? For you are a mist that appears for a little time and then vanishes."*

I remember, at age nine, after being told off by my parents, sitting in my bedroom vexed, saying to myself, "I can't wait till I'm big then no one can tell me what to do." Years later, the memory is clear as day, suddenly time has passed and I am BIG! *Realisation!* I don't have time to waste.....Time is, but waits for no one. Only God stays constant. He is the same yesterday, today and forever. In the meantime, I am learning to treasure every God given moment of life and live in hope and pray for longevity to fulfil my divine purpose and be a pleasing blessing that causes Him to shine on me.

TIME!

Time is a delicacy, handle with care
Time if not cherished, will disintegrate
It will disappear in plain sight, with eyes wide open
Time will catch up with, and outrun you
It will bypass and leave you standing in wonderment of its
distance
Time, master of itself, clock with its own destiny
Answers only to it's here then gone
Has no reason to wait for, or wait on you
Time is on a mission, it will continue with
or without you.

Time will see you born, watch you die,
boxed and buried
And if not written on paper, will forget about you
Occasionally, Time may pause in remembrance, but will
continue on track

Time is intolerant with stuckness and won't seek forgiveness
for leaving you behind
Time is precious, its main focus is to be used wisely
It will leave those who choose to waste it
It is impatient with idleness and won't converse
with procrastination
Plead stop, but Time won't wait, its interest
is invested in movement
Its delight is in the action of proactiveness.

Time has no jokes
Its laughter is the useful meditation of progress
Momentarily, it pauses to reflect on its history

And smiles at the pursuit of purpose
It lavishes in the stories of growth
Especially those of realisation of get up and go
Time becomes a little tearful with resolved baggage
And embraces speedy catch-up,
but waits not on regrets
For Time has a meeting with next day,
and sight-seeing with future.

Time is a delicacy, an acquired taste to be savoured
Like a beautiful butterfly, here today, gone tomorrow
Use it well, it will bring you unexpected favours
Time's mistreatment will knock you senseless
May leave you with pain, heart-scars
and permanent bruises
Time is a healer, brings medicine
to the wound, if you move
The movement of Time pushes change
Time used well will propel you forward.

Time, a reminder we are but a breath
A moment, a passing shadow
A brief moment upon this earth
Do today, tomorrow never a promise
Time has neither beginning or ending
No respecter of age or gender
Refuses to slow down to please
Time moves only forward, looks neither right nor left
Its only task, to impart wisdom
Its only hope, to transform you daily.

Time, like the dawning of the morning
It rises in the east and sets in the west
Nightfall, it travels to the north and roams the south

Time waits for no one, and takes no prisoners
It takes no thought for today, and has
no worries about tomorrow
It makes no apology for its entrance or escape
It is future forerunner with a promise, only of its Maker's
eternity
Time is a delicacy, handle with care.

But about that day or hour no one knows, not even the angels
in heaven Nor the Son, but only the Father. Be on guard!
Be alert! You do not know when the TIME will come.
Mark 13:32-33

PAUSE! Take a moment to reflect!

More Time Thoughts

All the poems in this book have been written at a different period in my life. And I'm sure you are already aware they are written in various length and styles depending on what was going on for me and my season of thoughts. Today, yet again, I am thinking about time...I am having what I choose to call an autumn moment.

I love the seasons and I have learnt to enjoy each as it comes. But there was a time when I fell out with autumn or the fall, as many call it. The leaves were falling off the trees and everything just looked messy. The garden looked unkempt, the pavements needed sweeping, the roads seemed overly crowded with traffic. In fact, the whole place seemed dark. I remember driving home from work one evening thinking, 'what a mess', really despising autumn. I had no idea what was happening or why I was projecting so much discontentment on autumn, harvest time, it really didn't make any sense at all. Autumn is beautiful and colourful with carpets of leaves everywhere, it's a time for gathering and enjoying the produce of the summer. Autumn for me represents change. It's that transitional period of ending, resting and making preparation for the new.

I love trees, all the different shapes, sizes and textures, I find them fascinating. I get this picture in my mind that when they sway in the wind they are waving to God, giving Him praise. One thing I've learnt about trees is that in the autumn when they shed their leaves, they produce an anti-freeze that enables them to withstand the cold weather. They may look naked but they are fully prepared and clothed for the winter.

Sorry I digressed! Back to my fallout with autumn.

Right now, my particular autumn moment is reflective of what appears to be a real messy season for me. My mind feels hoarded...I'm trying, but nothing appears to be coming to fruition. There is just so much stuff to do. I'm listening...I am not without encouraging voices or information and time is just passing me by...always transitioning but never coming into the fullness of transition. Yet even in my reflective messy thoughts, I know Lord, You are more than able. The fruits of summer begin in the dying of autumn.

Autumn Moments

Abba my God my King
Please hear the cry of my heart today
I am over-whelmed in the midst of my thoughts
My flesh wanting to amputate Your Spirit from my soul
My knowing better, wanting a fight
I am holding onto You in my season of despair
Time passing by…
Autumn again, winter season to go
I cannot afford to let You go…Holding on
I look outside at the frosted tree, leaves striped,
barks exposed
Its outside freeze is my inside bare
So full but seemingly going nowhere
Doing but never getting done
I look around my room, so much to be grateful for
My position better than most
Yet I can't help but wonder, will my time come?
Time passing by…
When will my summer come?
Hope thou in the Lord the Psalmist would say;
Autumn in here again…progress seems
to be passing me by
Better days are coming; hope thou in the Lord!
Soul look up! See where your help comes from
This autumn season, it too shall pass…

To everything there is a season
And a time to every purpose under heaven
Ecclesiastes 3:1KJV

I guess most of us have heard the well-known story about the Alabaster box.

Well if you haven't, you will find it in the gospels of *Matthew 26: 7-13 and Luke 7:37-38.* The story is about a woman who broke a bottle of expensive perfume, poured it over Jesus, used her tears to wash His feet and her hair to dry them. This act angered the disciples and religious leaders. They believed and complained that the perfume was far too costly to be wasted on Jesus. Their preference was to sell the perfume to make money; their concern for the poor is neither here nor there, they were just vexed with what they envisaged as wastage.

Over the years I have heard so many messages around the story about this unknown woman, but I would like to tell it AGAIN, one more time, according to my understanding. Additionally, you may also like to re-analyse it and make your own interpretation.

What really took place in that room on that day?

It must have been significantly important to Jesus because in the midst of his disciples' disgust, He said, *"Truly I tell you, wherever this gospel is preached throughout the world, what she has done will also be told, in memory of her."* What a statement! You can't tell me that you wouldn't be ecstatic to hear that your legacy is going to gain historical recognition for centuries to come. To this day, we are still discussing the love and generosity of this woman.

Let's take a closer look as to why Jesus put such emphasis on her!

Jesus was sat having supper with a group of men, if any women were present, they would have been serving the men. In the middle of these men (who would possibly have been highly focussed on debating current affairs), this strange woman, *no invitation,* dared to enter the room. As if that wasn't bad enough, she brazenly walked over and touched Jesus. She touched the man of God, the rabbi, the master, the teacher. Then she had the nerve to open a bottle of costly ointment and pour it over Him. **Listen to this bit:** as if things couldn't get worse, she got on the floor and began to kiss His feet, *how rude!* In the process of kissing His feet she began to cry. When His feet were soaking with her tears, she did the most disgraceful thing, she let her hair down and began to dry them. Can you visualise the shock in the room?

The reason I am dissecting the story is because I really want you to get the significance of what actually took place in the room. Here was a woman who the bible refers to as a sinner. Again, I emphasise, uninvited, walking into a house where she was not welcome. The men in the house were horrified when she walked in. Picture the scene, the hush, the whispers, the side eye. "What is she doing here? Isn't she the whore from down the street?"

I can imagine every tongue was rehearsing her past with scorn. How she came about owning an alabaster box was hot gossip. In bible days, unless you were wealthy or leading an immoral life you would not have possessed such an expensive item. Not only did she have the alabaster box, it was filled with a perfume called spikenard, a precious gift of great value. One of the men in the room commented, "If He, (meaning Jesus) was a prophet He would have known what sort of woman was touching Him." *(Luke 7:39).* The man was appalled.

My goodness, when religious folks ostracise you!

In biblical times a woman either covered her hair or wore it up in a bun; her hair was privy to herself or her husband. Unless she was a woman of the world (prostitute) she did not let it loose in public. The strict purity law of the land would suggest that her close proximity to Jesus, the act of touching Him in such a very intimate way, was worthy of death; What she did was considered shameful. A woman with her uncovered head in ancient bible times was deemed as seductive, almost as though she was naked. Yet this nameless woman, with extraordinary love, was prepared to take her chances in breaking the law. Possibly it was the first time in her life that she was genuinely accepted by a man who appreciated her without wanting anything more than just to renew and bring out the best in her...Unconditional love. The reaction from Jesus to this woman I believe, was revolutionary for its time.

My daughter just said, so much for equality!

Do you like essential oils? I do, they have so many health benefits. The perfume in the alabaster box, Spikenard, is also called Sweet Surrender. It is a highly scented oil known for its therapeutic properties in healing. Traditionally, it is used to relieve stress, tension, to calm the nerves, promote restful sleep and a relief for emotional pain.

What the disciples missed, was not only this woman's incredible love for Jesus but that she was preparing Him for His burial. She was providing emotional support for the mental impact and traumatic pain He was about to endure on the cross.

As human beings, we have a tendency to judge each other by the past and appearance - Jesus looks deeper. He looks at the heart. Despite those who were ridiculing her, she bowed down in reverence and kissed the feet of her Lord; *sometimes we just need to practice the fine art of humble kneeology.* The woman with the alabaster box denied her pride and bowed down in honour of her King.

In conclusion, I tell you this, it does not matter who you are, where you've come from, what you have done, or where you are at in life. It really doesn't matter what others are saying or have said about you. If you accept Jesus Christ as your Lord and Saviour and you are sincere, He is faithful and just to forgive you. *(1John1:9)* He will transform your life. He will never let you down.

This much I have observed about Christian life: people are only truly free when they find freedom in Christ. It is that same freedom that caused an ordinary woman to do something so selfless. Her legacy is a memorial to this day, just as Jesus declared over 2000 years ago.

ALABASTER BOX

My true Love
He loves me beyond measure
He who has sanctified and purified me
in the midst of them that oppose me
Those who are merciless and despise me
My true Love, as I stretch forth my heart to You
show Yourself strong in my defence.

Open the door of my soul O King
It is not locked, You are free to come in
Take Your residence here within
Sit upon the throne of my spirit
Come my Love, let me anoint Your head
with oil from the alabaster box of my soul.

Come now my Desire
Let me was wash Your feet
with the perfume of my tears
Let me dry between Your toes with my hair
Yes, I will kiss and caress You
Let them look
Them who scorn me, let them watch.

Come now my Love
Let us embrace
Let our spirits connect
Let the intimacy of our oneness be so.
Inhale my Love, breathe deep through Your nostrils
Smell the fragrance of the oil
flowing from the alabaster box of my soul.

My Love, let them have an open view
Yes! Them who ostracise me
Let them witness the affection of my Beloved
as You reciprocate my love.
Let them who choose to ridicule me
Let them see love invested, sustained in unity.

My Love, my Lord
Put them in wonderment of Your faithfulness to me
Come my Love, ignite me with the flames
of Your compassion
Feel the warmth, the scented aroma
in the atmosphere
Let me massage You with the oil from
the alabaster box
overflowing and mingled with tears collected from
the centre of my being.

Save me my King, save me
Save me from those who seek to take my life
Let them see Your passionate emotions for me
Let them see our binding tenderness...UNSPOKEN!
Let them fear my Eternal One.

My Beloved, my Lover, my King
Let them see You seated high upon Your Throne
Let them behold You, anointed with costly oil
Give them, those who object to our love
Give them full view of Your glory
Let them see He who is my life source
Adorned in the essence of holiness
Saturated with oil from the alabaster box of my heart.

When a certain immoral woman from the city heard
He was eating there, she brought a beautiful
alabaster jar filled with expensive perfume.
Then she knelt behind Him at His feet, and she
wiped them off with her hair.
Then she kept kissing His feet and
putting perfume on them.
Luke 7:37:38 NLT

Due to my very strict and harsh upbringing, I learnt at an early age not to smile. As a child I also learnt to be seen and not heard. It helped to stop some of the severe beatings and emotional trauma. By the time I was old enough to leave home, aged 16, I was a bitter, angry and blunt young person. If you bothered me, I was prepared to take you out. I never ran from any situation or anyone....Mind you, I still don't run from anyone now...I refuse to live in fear of anyone, world or church people. No one bullies me...if the God I serve doesn't bully me, you cannot either. I don't get caught-up with clergy superiority. Whilst I respect called leaders, I am not going allow church titles to intimidate me, many have tried. I firmly believe that respect is earned not demanded. If you're not Jesus I am not kissing your feet. If you treat your flock right, they will follow you all the way to the water and back.

Breathe...Its okay...I am much more subdued today. God has a way of moulding and refining the clay. Like you I am a work in progress. When I gave my life to Christ, my older brother, Neville, even though he wasn't a Christian, was relieved. His thoughts were, his sister was safe. As far as he was concerned, Christianity prevented me killing someone and ending up behind bars or being killed, because I would prefer to fight rather than take flight.

Oh dear! At the start of my Christian life, church was not my cup of tea. Church folks were just weird, unrealistic. I couldn't get my head around the passiveness; everyone was so perfectly subservient. I was spilt, half of me in the church the other half out in the world. I just couldn't make the transition. Some Sunday evenings I left the service and straight to blues (Very dark party, with heavy bass-line music that finished around 4am in the morning). I continued my double life until one night I was in a blues as usual, standing between the speaker boxes as always. I didn't dance, just always stood by the speakers, allowing the rhythm of the bass to go through me...dodum, dodum, dum, dum, dum. I was in a world of my own. SUDDENLY, I heard the Lord say, "You shouldn't be in here." I left and never turned back since.

I continued going to church but something was missing from my life. It was frustrating because I didn't know what that something was or how to find it. The ignorant preaching at the time did not help me. It assumed that once you gave your life to Christ you were perfect. There was no room for error, mistake was frowned upon. *So far from the truth,* life is a journey. When we give our lives to Christ, we change roads, but we still have to grow and overcome the obstacles in life like anyone else. The only difference is, we are anchored in the hope of eternal life. We have divine protection but we are still faced with the reality of life and everything it throws at us.

Giving your life to Christ is just the beginning. From there on, you begin a journey of transformational change, which admittedly, was a real slow process for me. God bless you if you have spent your life in church since day dot, and have always conformed to the protocol of perfection. SORRY, that is not my story. I am the rebel from outside the wall who couldn't shift her anger. I didn't do fake, so couldn't join everyone with the Cheshire cat smiles. I could not work out why or what everyone was smiling about; it just did not make sense. To make matter worse, you know you always get one interfering person in church, well, her name was Dawnell Jones. She was the original pain in the neck; Lord Have Mercy; Goodness me...CHURCH PEOPLE!

Growing up, my parents never hugged or showed me any affection and I hated...again I emphasise, I HATED touch. I associated touch with doing something wrong or getting a beating. Whenever someone in church approached me, my facial expression would tell them to back off. However, Dawnell was never deterred by this. Whilst everyone else saw me as a fire breathing dragon, she recognised the hurting child who needed a hug - I didn't even recognise that myself. I had no idea I was emotionally scarred and in pain. Unfortunately, not every Christian has been blessed with the gift of discernment. Every time I walked in church, she would hug me tight, tight, real tight. I would get really mad, but she was so thick skinned, she totally ignored my vexation. Every week she upset me by insisting on hugging me. It did not matter what I said to her, the following week she would be at the door to hug me again.

Things took a dramatic change that still impacts my life today (Tearful). I enjoyed the evening services at church, it was a time of testimony and reflection. It was more intimate and besides, there were less people. One evening Dawnell got up and gave her testimony, after listening attentively to her story, it felt as though someone lifted a huge burden from my shoulders. I felt a great sense of relief. Someone knew my story; someone had lived it. No wonder she refused to give up on me. As a result of her testimony I learnt to hug her back. God used her to teach me how to receive and give affection. It was okay to allow people to love me and it was okay for me to love me. It's okay.

What I learnt from this experience is you can't tell a story if you've not done the journey. Familiarity connects to familiarity.

The next poem is a reminder of a song Dawnell always walked around church singing...I'm Yours Lord:

I'M YOURS

I'm Yours Lord
Everything I am,
I'm Yours
All of my heart;
I'm Yours
All of my soul,
I'm Yours
All of my body,
I'm Yours
All of my mind,
I'm Yours
Try me now and see I'm completely Yours.
I'm Yours Lord
In all things,
I'm Yours
In every situation
I'm Yours
Regardless of,
I'm Yours
My inner and outer being
I'm Yours
Always and forever
I'm yours
Look and see Lord, I am completely Yours.

O God You are my God; earnestly I seek You; my soul thirsts for You; My flesh faints for You, as in a dry weary land where there is no water.
Psalm 63:1 ESV

Have you ever woken up really excited about Jesus? No apparent reason, you just have a lightbulb moment where you are experiencing Him in an unusual way. You feel a newness in how you perceive Him and you want to let Him know how much He means to you. You just feel excited and want to tell the world how good He has been to you.

The Next Poem in about one of those extra special delightful days.

DELIGHTED IN HIM

When I delight myself in Him,
He is faithful to fulfil my dreams
I commit my life to Him, trust Him
wholeheartedly to bring my desires to pass
I take my rest in Him, excellent is His
mercy towards me
I am so in love with Him; wrapped up,
tied up, bundled up in ecstasy.
Surely, I can declare that He is my truth.
A pleasure it is to have my footsteps ordered by Him
In reverential fear I cleanse the runway
of my life for Him to make His approach
The grit and grime, my best I try,
to thoroughly clean for His arrival.
I cast aside every thought and imagination that
propose to exalt itself above Him.

Him I know is a consuming incinerator;
with His wings He overshadows me as
His radioactive light burns the stubborn
stains of debris...residue found within.
Oh! That He can take His place, creating
soundness inside my bones.
I need not fret for He is my hiding feathers
of grace; arms grasped tightly around me.
In Him I am comforted, fervent protection
from the adversary.
O that I am absorbed in Him... YES...!
Truly I am blessed.

Such is the explosion in my inward parts -
I cannot contain; I must tell the world of my
destiny of hope in the great divine.

Perfect is His love for me, to Him I sacrifice my soul.
I have no fear in handing ME to Him.
My heart takes its rest in His bosom, for I am assured He will
not drop it, but caress it against His own.
My refuge, my strength, my much-assisted help,
in past, present and future.
I am honoured to have Him reign in my
innermost being.
Oh, how excellent is His greatness; how
beautiful, how marvellous, how amazingly magnificent.
How awesome is the King of Zion.
Humbly, I enrich myself in His glory, for
in victory He is high and lifted up.
With gladness I rejoice; with thanksgiving
I give Him praise.

With adoration I worship Him in
the beauty of His holiness.
I cleave to the joy of knowing Him.
I prosper in the intimacy of His wholeness.
I cling to the sceptre in His right hand, He bid me come, will
never let me go; My faith I place entirely in Him. I pull forth the
evidence of my prayers and expose His miracles to the world.
Great pleasure I take in upholding Him for all to see
Then they will know, My KING, the everlasting one,
FOR REAL, He was and He is and He is to come.

But seek ye first the kingdom of God, and His righteousness;
and all these things shall be added unto you.
Matthew 6:33 KJV

UNCONDITIONAL LOVE

My faith is in Him who first loved me
In Him is my hope
Just as I am, He called me
Chose me just as I am
Fervent is His love for me
I am comforted in Him.

Sincere is His love for me
My faults are unseen
Accepted just as I am
Loved for who I am
Amazing His Grace
Sought me out... found me
Lost sheep...
Unconditional love.

But God who is rich in mercy, for His great love where with He loved us
Ephesians 2:4 KJV

Some years ago, I was having a conversation with a friend. I'm not quite sure what we were talking about, but I can distinctly remember her saying, "When we refuse to appreciate who we are, we are telling God that He got it wrong about us." What are your thoughts about this?

In today's society, the cosmetic industry, designer labels, social media, celebrity status, other people's judgements and opinions appear to dictate who we are, who we should be and how we should change to fit into the mould of acceptance. The falseness on social platforms has become the teachers and standards to live by. Tactless critics decide whether or not we fit the stereotypical image of someone worthy of presence. People are no longer content to be the person who they were born to be, every defect has to be fixed. Everyone seems to be striving for the perfect body, perfect face and, if they are not body-perfect, they create their own ideal of difference with body-art (I'm not quite sure what perfect is). It feels like madness in the name of beauty and the need to be seen. So many people have fallen out with themselves because they do not consider themselves good enough to be who they are *(Don't get me wrong I have those days)*. Social anxiety, depression, panic and the big one for me... Social-Like Rejection, reinforce the feeling of failure and the feeling of being non-desirable.

I remember my daughter, aged 14 years at the time, coming home from school quite frustrated. In her annoyance she said, "Mum, I don't care what anybody thinks about me. I am going to be who I am." She went on to say, "If you are fat or skinny, you get called names; if you are black or white, you get called names, if you are intelligent or not you get called names." She said, "Mum it doesn't matter who you are or what you do you still get called names; you can't win. So, you know what? I like Me just the way I am!"

The next poem is dedicated to everyone who does not know or has forgotten who they are. I encourage you to begin to create a relationship with YOU. Look in the mirror right now, look into your eyes and say these words...**I LIKE ME!** Know today that you are a beautiful child of the King who sits in heavenly places, the one who in the beginning said, "Let us make man in our image, after our likeness (Genesis 1:26 KJV).

Keep looking in the mirror and repeat:

**I AM MADE IN THE IMAGE
AND LIKENESS OF GOD
...SO I LIKE ME!**

I LIKE ME

I like me
I like me because I am nice
I like me because I am very nice
I like me because I am very nice nice
I like me because I am very nice nice nice
I like me because I am absolutely nice nice,
I like me because I am absolutely wonderfully nice
I like me because I am sooooooooo absolutely wonderfully nice
I like me because I am soooooo absolutely wonderfully scrumptiously nice
I like me because I am soooooo absolutely, wonderfully, scrumptiously, beautifully, delightfully, gorgeously, brilliantly, fantastically, magnificently, tremendously, exquisitely, adorably, extremely, amazingly, marvellously, terrifically, excellently, fabulously, incredibly, exceptionally, lovingly, positively

N....I....C....E!

Before I formed you in the belly I knew you; and before you came forth out of the womb I sanctified you, and I ordained you a prophet onto the nations.
Jeremiah 1: 5 KJV

This is a Serious Crossroad...

Be sure you're on the right path. The reason I say this is because the next poem is called Truth. I wrote it as a means of relieving the pain I was feeling at the time. As I have become more intimate with God, I have learnt to be careful who I allow to minister to me, especially when it comes to the laying on of hands. People are not always who they say they are. Wisdom has taught me the importance of spiritual discernment. Just because someone claims to be a pastor, apostle, evangelist, prophet, doesn't mean they are anointed. The bible urges us to not just *believe, but try the spirits whether they are of God because false prophets have gone out into the world. (1John 4:1)* Jesus Christ is called the Truth - He never condemns. He is the restorer of life.

Some years ago, I allowed someone to lay hands on me and when he finished praying, I was immobilised for two years. They were the worst two years of my life. He devastated me, leading me to believe I wasn't good enough to be called a child of God - my prayers were not good enough to be heard. To be honest, he made me feel like worthless scum. Unknowing to others, at that time, I became quite dysfunctional. As a counsellor, I was struggling to meet the needs of my clients. I survived at work because a Christian colleague from another project, when I explained to her what had happened, just interceded for me. Apart from my husband, she was the only one who knew what was going on for me. Although they both encouraged me, for some reason I was unable to function or overcome my suicidal thoughts. I have been through low periods in my life, but that particular season was an horrendous nightmare. No joke, in those two years, if I had died I would not have cared...mind you if I die, I wouldn't know I was dead!

NEVER AGAIN!

You may say Esha, why are you telling me all this? What's your point? What has this story got to do with reading the book? Let me tell you, this is a book about the unlimited, untarnished, pure love of the King. I am telling you this story because many times we fail to see the bigness of God and the love He has extended to us. When you avoid drawing close to Him, when you refuse to read His word, when you don't know who you are in Him, when you have no real understanding that He is no respecter of persons, then someone with a clergy title littered with wrong motives will come along and mentally paralyse you. The word of God declares, 'who the Son has set free is free indeed' (John 8 :36). Jesus loves you unconditionally. *Therefore if any man be in Christ, he is a new creature: old things are passed away; behold all things are become new. (2 Corinthians 5 :17) KJV.*

Know that: *Greater love has no man than this, than a man lay down his life for his friends (John 15 :13).* No church leader did that for you, JESUS DID, JESUSSS! Know this also, *as I recently learnt this in a seminar,* if the God above with all His attributes, He who gives life and takes away life - if He is not condemning you, what do you care what anybody else says about you? Hey! I don't know who I am speaking to here, but somebody who's going through something similar needs to receive this. Let the TRUTH speak to you.

TRUTH

God the Father, God the King,
God the Creator, God the Saviour
He is the **Truth**
Truth is a bleach it shows you who you really are
Truth hurts without demoralising.
The hurt of **Truth** will set you free,
not keep you in bondage.
Truth opens the door, not slam it shut.
The pains of **Truth** open the door to life.
Truth brings understanding, which affects change.
Truth is honest, it is not vindictive.
Its only purpose is to affect change
for the good of the individual.
Truth is empathetic, it has no alternate motives.
It doesn't set out to maim or paralyse.
It is not insensitive, has no score to settle.
Being right is not important to **Truth.**
The main aim of **Truth** is to impart knowledge.
Truth introduces you to wisdom
Truth draws a person's attention to areas of weaknesses in
their life.
Truth assists positive change.
Truth is not abrasive.
It operates in the comfort of love.
The words of **Truth** are pure and clear, straight but
compassionate.
Truth is justice without condemnation.
Truth never belittles or allows you to fall,
Instead, it will lift you up and create
an atmosphere of sensibility.
Truth will never hold your past against you.

Truth will reflect your past of negativity
In addition, use it to build your future.
Truth is never inappropriate.
It is considerate and timely.
Truth is not proud or grudgeful. It is not legalistic.
Truth exercises authority without destruction.
Truth is sometimes stern but it knows
how to carry a smile.
Truth is both huggable and durable.
Truth never exposes you wrongly, it will protect you.
Truth is interested in your safety and peace of mind.
Truth will set you free!

When the Spirit of truth comes, He will guide you in all truth.
He will not speak of His own but will tell what He has heard.
He will tell you about the future
John 16:13

MY AMAZING GRACE

"Bless the Lord O my soul
And 'ALL' that is within me
Bless His Holy Name" Psalm 103:1

I will bless Him My Lover
My Amazing Grace
My soul, I call on you to
magnify Him
My spirit, I call on you to
worship Him.

"I will bless the Lord at all times
His praise shall continually
Be in my mouth" Psalm 34:1

I will bless Him My Lover
Forever and always
My ears, I call on you to
hear the distinctiveness of His voice
My mouth, I call on you to
prophesy, call His word into being.

"I will lift up mine eyes unto the hills
From where comes my help" Psalm121:1

I will bless Him My Lover
My eyes, I call on you to
set your sight straight way upon Him
My feet, I call on you to
walk His pathway of light.
"Glory ye in His Holy Name: Let

The heart of them rejoice that
Seek the Lord" Psalm 105:3

I will bless Him My Lover
My hands, I call on you to
be lifted in His Name
Heart, I call on you to
pour out your affection before Him
BODY! I call on you to
drench in the fullness of His glory.

Let everything that has breath
praise the Lord. Praise the Lord!
Psalm 150 (NKJV)

The next poem overwhelms me. It really has had an impact on me. I wrote it then I had to sit and reflect on what I had written. The God I love, my heavenly Father, the righteous God of justice commands that I love my neighbour as I love myself. That's okay. Then guess what? He also expects me to pray for my enemies and those people who sometimes hurt me, even the treacherous calculating deviants I so often want to evict from society. Despite my feelings, He wants me to pray for change. He hates the sin but loves the man; He really is impartial. I must admit, it is hard and seems unfair to comprehend that when bad people give their hearts to Christ, He is faithful and just to forgive them. Unlike man, not only does He look beyond the faults and sees the needs, He is able to set the captives free. His love is immeasurable.

What a mighty God we serve! I don't get it: How can you not love Him? He gives everyone chance and opportunity. He rains on the just and on the unjust. Hardly seems fair, but My King is a God whose throne is built on righteousness and justice. Until His return, He gives hope to all. He protects His own while waiting or those coming to find His heart of forgiveness.

GOD'S COUNSEL

God's counsel reflects the wisdom of life
It goes deeper than the surface of self.
It searches the depth of the soul and reveals
the true condition of the heart.

God's counsel rejuvenates the mind
it evicts negative thoughts.
It exposes the pains and hurts that
so often, cause us to doubt Him.

God's counsel heals the wounds of despair.
It is the light of wisdom and restoration.
It brightens the darkest valleys and
revives the spirit on the loneliest walks.

The counsel of God in all its wisdom and power
will convict and purify the most
treacherous and murderous mind.
His forgiveness will rub out any crime
His transformation of beauty is phenomenal.

The counsel of the world develops,
brings temporal understanding
to a problematic situation in a person's life.
However, the world's psychology
at its best is no comparison
to the depth and counsel of the Most High God.

For my thoughts are not your thoughts, neither
are your ways my ways, says the Lord.
Isaiah 55: 8 KJV

Look in the Mirror

Anyone who knows me today, would never believe there was a time when I couldn't really look in the mirror. I didn't like the person on the other side looking back at me, so where possible, I just avoided mirrors. Growing up, no one ever told me that I was beautiful, so I just imagined that I was a nasty, ugly, bad person, who just could not do anything right for anyone.

Isn't it interesting that children who have been emotionally rejected and criticised all their lives grow up tapping into the self-fulfilling prophecy of low self- esteem and poor self-image, having no sense of self or any real direction in life? You get up every morning, put on your mask and enter another day of pretence; no one the wiser that you are screaming in agony inside.

Today, I realise that I have spent a very long time pity-partying. I have wasted many years trying to be who other people wanted me to be; trying to mould me, reshape me. I couldn't meet my parents' standards and I didn't meet the criteria of the holy church girl; someone from church once called me the street gal...How easy it is for some people to forget where they're coming from.

Bishop T.D Jakes once said "There is nothing like when church folks curse you."

Now that I am in relationship with my King, now that He has taken residence inside me, now that God my salvation...Yahweh Ro'eh, my Shepherd, now that He sits on the pinnacle of my soul, and is there to guide me in all truth, now that His wisdom has become my key...LISTEN!

Can't Touch This
Heyyy!
...Attitude...

You, Yes YOU! Today, begin to look in the mirror and get acquainted with who you are; see yourself as God sees you. His prized possession designed and equipped with His Greatness seed!

WHEN I LOOK IN THE MIRROR.

What do I see?
When I look in the mirror
What do I see?
I see a child of Zion
Princess beautiful
Daughter of the Most High God.

What do I see?
When I look in the mirror
I see the reflection of His Supreme Majesty
King of kings...Lord of lords.
Conquering lion from the tribe of Judah.

What do I see?
When I look in the mirror
What do I see?
I see the beauty of His Amazing Grace
The glory of His righteousness.

What do I see?
When I look in the mirror
What do I see?
I see the creative thoughts of His Mind
The artistic vision of my Creator.

What do I see?
When I look in the mirror
What do I see?
I see the heart of my King
The holiness of His Spirit
The essence of His breath.

What do I see?
When I look in the mirror
What do I see?
I see the creation of a living soul
The careful structure of a potter's hands
A vessel of clay delicately formed.

What do I see?
When I look in the mirror
What do I see?
I see the compassion of a Father
Unconditional love beyond measure.

What do I see?
When I look in the mirror
What do I see?
I see the image of the One True God
Silent eyes with a loud voice whispering
You are fearfully and wonderfully made.

I praise You: for I am fearfully and wonderfully made:
Marvellous are You works; and that my soul knows right well.
Psalm 13 :14 KJV

REFLECTION IN THE MIRROR

It is good to look in the mirror and
see yourself as God sees you
Look in the mirror and fall in love with yourself
Know that you have been intricately designed
You are the essence of loveliness.
Look in the mirror and take an artistic interest in you
With assurance, stand tall.
Look in the mirror and see the excellence of God
You are the imagination of His mind given life
Know that you are His greatest creation
made in His image
Crafted with precision and shaped with love
The mirror is your truth; it tells no lies.

Look in the mirror; do you not marvel
the identity of the living breath?
See the reflection of the EL ROI, the God who sees
Was it not Him who said to His Spirit and Son "Come let us make
man in our likeness"?
O, to know you resemble the I AM!

Was it not Him who stooped from the heavens, lowered Himself
to the ground?
Did He not stretch forth His hands
to the ground, mingled the soil?
Like a potter rotating his wheel,
did He not mould the dirt?
Did His hands not shape the mud and carved it through His
fingers until the form looked like Him?
A building of light extracted from darkness
Take a glance and see the prized possession
Look to see the sculptured trophy of victory.

Again, look in the mirror
Do you not recognise Him?
Look carefully at the outstanding architectural design
Constructed by Him, the Master Builder,
The one who fashioned you in the
moments of His mind
Even before the world began, were you
not the embryo of His thoughts?
For He lowered Himself from His throne.
Yes, it was He who kissed your lips,
with the breath of agreement
Blew the wind of love stimulating...YES
...circulating your inner emptiness
Bringing to existence a living being,
a manifestation of His great power
You...Yes You...sent to earth on purpose for a purpose
Even for such a time as this
Mighty are the works of His hands.

The Lord your God is in your midst, a mighty one who will save:
He will rejoice over you with gladness;
He will quiet you by His love;
He will exult over you with loud singing.
Zephaniah 3:17 ESV

ONE HUNDRED PERCENT.

My Lover is My best friend
He refuses to accept 99 per cent of my effort

He desires only the best for me
My friend, My Lover; He believes in me

He won't settle for My second best
He is My greatest admirer, hence

He seeks to extract 1 percent more
Thus enabling MY full potential

100 per cent

And to one he gave five talents,
to another two, and to another one; to
every man according to his ability.
Matthew 25:15 KJV

Have you ever had a day when your spirit was so overwhelmed with the goodness of God that you just needed time to pause, reflect and absorb what He has done for you?

You walk into church without a care in the world, you're bursting with joy and excitement. Your feet are dancing before you reach the door. You just want to praise Him. You don't need music to pump you up, you just want to worship Him.

It doesn't matter how boring the service is, whether or not the praise and worship team are out of tune, whether the pastor is preaching a sermon that you've heard a thousand and one times before, or the church secretary is giving some monotonous announcements. It really doesn't matter if the rest of the congregation think you're loud or plain crazy. You're so overcome with the passion of Christ and at that moment your heart is so connected to His heart, you just want to bless Him.

Like a remote control you just press...PAUSE!...Stop everything...so you can Magnify Him, Glorify Him, Exalt Him, and shout His name on High, give Him your Halleluyah...WHY... because deep down in your bowels you know that you are serving an indescribable God.

PAUSE!

Give me a moment O Lord
Let me dance around Your throne
Let me embrace the intimacy of Your Glory.

Pause!

Give me a moment to reflect on Your Goodness
Enter into Your presence with thanksgiving
in my heart
Walk through Your courts with feet
excited to praise You.

Pause!

Give me a moment to rejoice for the
gladness within my heart
Allow me to reach out and hug Your presence
Bask in the atmosphere of Your glory.

Pause!

Give me a moment to consider Your Greatness
Let my soul climb up to kiss Your lips
Breathe Lord, Breathe, let me feel Your Breath.

Pause!

Give me a moment to rest in Your Holiness
Let me reflect upon Your overflow of love for me
Let my imagination run wild my King.

Pause!

Give me a moment to absorb Your scent
Let me inhale deep and take You in
Let me rest my head against Your heartbeat
to hear it sing
...............................LISTENING..............................
I love to hear Your song of love about me
O how wonderful is my Saviour's love for me.

PAUSE!

In psalm 84 when the Psalmist's heart

touched God's heart he wrote, in verse two;

"My soul longeth, yea, even fainteth for

the courts of the Lord;

my heart and my flesh crieth out

for the living God" KJV

I Love Yellow Thorn Roses.

Did you know that if you break the thorns of roses you cause them to die quicker?
My research has taught me that the thorns on roses help them to absorb water. If you remove the thorns, they are unable to get enough water to keep them alive. If you don't believe me, try this test: buy two bunches of roses, one with thorns and one without thorns, see which one lives the longest.

I love thorn roses especially yellow ones, a vivid reminder of the plaited crown of thorns forced into the temples of my Lover's brow.

My husband only ever buys me Yellow Thorn Roses.
Because Roses with thorns are a reminder not to judge me from the outside. I am not prickly, I am very delicate, with a wonderful fragrance, so handle me with care.

Send a gift of Thorn Roses
to someone you care about!

YELLOW THORN ROSES

My Lover, He brings me Yellow Thorn Roses
Freshly picked from the garden of His heart
Sweetly scented, an aroma of love
Warm passionate a tender touch
Romance in His eyes a bitter sweet kiss
A bloody lip from an exotic rose
An acquired taste with a hint of blood.
I don't complain, the feeling's good
As a token of His love to light up my heart
My Lover, He brings me Yellow Thorn Roses.

I am the rose of Shar'on and the lily of the valleys.
Song of Solomon 2:1 KJV

A Gift to Abba!

Just imagine, Yeshua wants to present you to His Father absolutely perfect; no defects. On that great day, in your wedding gown, you are going to look stunning, even you would want to marry you. 'Seriously' can you see yourself being presented faultless, as though you had never sinned, in the fullness of purity before your Creator?

Do you really know how valuable you are?

You are PRICELESS, a gift bought with precious sacrificial blood, wrapped with mercy and sealed with grace. Know who you are; a bride being prepared for a King. Men! On that day you will experience the joys of being a bride.

I wonder if you dare to peek into the future and see yourself standing in the presence of the Lord, holy and acceptable in a garment of righteousness with a crown made of pure gold, possibly laden with jewels? If you are unable to visualise yourself being presented to God the Father, then right now prophesy it to yourself......I will...SPEAK IT!

If you are in a place where you are not sure if you're going to make it, just begin to work out your own salvation with fear and trembling. Stay with your Beloved for another season, trust in Him and He will make your salvation sure. It will be worth it when you lift your veil and behold Him face to face.

ENGAGED TO THE KING

My Lover,
He promised never to leave or forsake me
My Lover,
He said He loves me with an everlasting love
My Lover,
He is truth, He never lies
If He did not love me, He would have told me
My Lover,
Faithful is He, full of integrity
My Lover,
He promised to make me His bride
Array me in a garment of white with a golden crown
My Lover,
He promised to take me to His home beyond the sky
There to meet His Father and heavenly host
My Lover,
He has journeyed on ahead to prepare a place for me
My Lover,
A beautiful mansion He is building
Architecture structured for His chosen one
My Lover,
He promised a huge banquet on our wedding day
All the saints of earth will be there
To witness a marriage of eternity
My Lover,
He is trustworthy, true to His words
My Lover,
On that day He will present me
Tried and tested without spot or blemish
Pure, shinning as gold
A perfect bride to His Father.

DID YOU KNOW I AM ENGAGED TO THE KING?

That He might present it to Himself a glorious church, not having spot or wrinkle, or any such thing; but that it should be holy and without blemish.
Ephesians 5:27KJV

One of my most memorable moments of my childhood was growing up in the Caribbean amongst nature. Running freely in the beaming sun, barefoot and blue sky. Granny could never find me, busy catching fire flies. Just to think I was never afraid of the dark. When I think about it, light and darkness in the Caribbean was quite strange. There was almost no warning, it was light at 6.55pm and pitch darkness at 7pm; just like someone pressed a light switch and turned the light off. Then the crickets would liven up the bushes with their loudness; their voices singing the same song, every night. Almost like they were chanting, *"Today you had your fun, tonight it's our turn to 'PARTY.' "* Then the fire flies would light up the night with their twinkling, like earth night stars. As I think about it now, those were memorable life-story moments.

My King is inspirationally outstanding. He does all things well. His creation is miraculous. His attention to detail is so visible in each of His creatures, whether animal, bird, insect or fish. His creative beauty is clearly evident in His work. It is quite obvious why He is known as the...

Wonder of Wonders!

GLOW LIGHT

Oh Lord, My God, My King

Your Shekinah Glory is incomprehensible
In the cleft of the rock Moses could only glance
You shielded his eyes to only a backside view
To behold You in the power of Your light is death
Such is the beauty of Your Holiness.
Your train, Isaiah said, filled the temple of heaven
In his vision of You sitting on
Your throne Ezekiel describes
Your prestigious light,

The light shining around Him looked like the rainbow in the clouds on a day of rain. This was what the shining-greatness of what the Lord looked like.

Ezekiel 1:28 NLV

My God My King, My Lord

I can hardly find words to describe how
nature reveals You
Like the firefly lighting up the dark night
Help me to flicker a flame into someone's darkness
To light up their life to see that You are the only
HOPE in this world of despair

My King, My Lord, My God

Let Your glow in me be the light that plants a seed
of Your goodness, Your greatness,
Your passion, to help transform a soul
To connect to Your heart in spirit and truth.

Oh Lord, My God, My King
In this world of distress and worry
Allow Your light to flow through me
to leave a trail of soundness to a stressful mind
to follow the narrow road and be
the few that find You.

My God, My King, My Lord
Like the firefly lighting up the midnight sky
make me a glow of light in the lives of others
So that Your brightness in me can
brighten up their world
Cause them to smile at the storm
Command it be still.

My King, My Lord, My God
Lord, make me a glow of light in the dark
Lord, enable me to shine in the lives of others
Calling their own light into being
So they can see clearly, come to know You
and be transformed into a shining
star to light another.

Oh Lord, My God, My King
As I draw from Your lighthouse each morning
make me a catalyst to project Your glory in this world
Allow Your lovingkindness to shine through my life
So that others may see and offer You
a sacrifice of praise.

Let your light shine before men, that they may see your good works,
and glorify your Father which is in heaven.
Matthews 5:16 KJV

Words of Encouragement...

God is never looking for highfalutin words, elaborate well-rehearsed bible scholars, or leadership hierarchy. He is just looking for a heart and mind that are obedient, teachable and receptive to His Holy Spirit. He is looking for communication; just plain and simple talk between you and Him. Many times in the mornings, I just sit on my sofa and have a heart and thought conversation with Him. Sometimes I make sense and other times I get really silly and say the most ridiculous things, or just ask lots of questions, or just simply pray a really mixed up prayer that He has to untangle. This is how it goes sometimes ...

Lord, You are not a man so You don't lie
Your Word is Your Bond
It never fails, it stands forever
Your Word Lord, will always accomplish what You have spoken
It will never come back to You empty
Lord Your Word is True
That is why, today I can...
gird up my waist with Your belt of Truth...
and it will stay firm and never come loose
Lord, Your Word is sacred
It is impossible for You to lie
You are full of integrity
Your Word is Yes and Amen
Lord, You never waiver, You are a constant temperature
You are never lukewarm
You are never in-between
Your Word is either or neither
Your Word Lord is firm and sure
Your Word always hits its target
Your Word is truthful and just
No wonder in Psalm 119:11 David said...

Your Word I have hidden in my heart that I will not sin against You
Lord, today, I too hide your word in my heart that I may not sin against You
I stand on Your Word
I trust Your Word
As Isaiah wrote...
"People are like the grass and flowers: their beauty comes up then it fades but the Word of God is vibrant and strong, it stands forever."
Bless Your Name Lord. Bless Your Name
Thank You for the beauty of Your Holiness.
Amen

"For the Word of God is alive and active. Sharper than any double-edged sword, it penetrates even to dividing soul and spirit, joints and marrow: it judges the thoughts and attitudes of the hearts."
Hebrews 4:12 NIV

Another day I will sit in the same spot, get out my notebook and
write my thoughts like this...

Lord You are so amazing.
You have this wonderful relationship with nature.
Even the inanimate objects have life in You.
Lord You can communicate with any still life
You can raise the rocks to life to praise You!
You can bring anything into existence.
Even the darkness respects and bows to Your light
Your presence is like heaven on earth.
It exposes the dark.
You have a relationship with the sun,
the moon and the stars.
The earth is crying for You...For it knows who You are.

The atmosphere and all the atoms and
particles know who You are.
The laws of nature know how to give You praise because it
recognises Your infinite beauty.
Oh that men will not fail to recognise You
Oh that men will reverence the God
of purity and holiness.
Oh that Your people will come to know of Your sovereignty and
worship at Your feet.
Oh that they will recognise the sacrifice
of Your Son, Yeshua.
Oh that they will acknowledge the intercessory prayer in
heaven for us, day and night, because
You never get sleepy or doze.
You watch over us like an eagle watching
over her unhatched chicks
You spread Your arms like wings to shelter
us from the storms of life.

In You Lord, I have my life. I can run to
You and find safety.
To Adonai who blesses our going out and coming in,
Our divine protector, Your church Almighty God,
is the apple of Your eyes.
Lord You love us so much that You allowed Your Son
to be beaten, spat on, nailed to a cross,
thirst, pierced with a sword.
He was humiliated beyond recognition for us...mankind

WHAT A MIGHTY GOD YOU ARE!!!

My Lord, my heavenly Father, no one, nothing in heaven, on
earth, under the earth, can
compare to You...NOTHING...
You are incomparable, indescribable, awesome, undisputable
powerful, great and mighty.
I am so privileged...Blessed to be called Your child.

See Lord, I always put You in Capitals, You're just far too BIG to
do lowercase.
In Jesus Name
Amen
CRAZZZZY.............YES I KNOW!

I will give thanks to You, Lord, with all my heart;
I will tell of all Your wonderful deeds
Psalm 9:1KJV

Other days it goes like this...

Good morning Lord
Good morning Jesus
Good Morning Holy Spirit
Good Morning all Host of heaven

Crazy I know but that's how it goes sometimes.
I blew Him a kiss...Sometimes three kisses...
Ummmah, Ummmah, Ummmah!

Lord thank You for waking me up this morning
Waking me up is enough for me to give You praise

Many people went to sleep last night and
never made it today
So Lord I give You thanks. It's not my
breath but Yours, on loan to me.

Lord today, I come in agreement with
Jeremiah when He recalled...
'It is of the Lord's mercies that we are not consumed,
because His compassion fails not. They are new
every morning: great is thy faithfulness.
Lamentations 3 v 22-23 KJV

Indeed, Lord Your steadfast love
never comes to an end.
Thank You for Your mercies towards me. Thank You.
I am so grateful to You, simply for not giving up on me
And not allowing me to give up on me.
I love You Lord...only You...Your grace and mercy!

The Lord says, "I will rescue those who love Me.
I will protect those who trust in My Name.
Psalm 91:14 NLT

My Lover & My King
The Lord God of Yisrael

WHO IS HE?
Who is the God of Abraham and Isaac and Jacob?
Who is the God that I am so ecstatic about?

?

YHWH...I AM

I AM THAT I AM

YHWH ELOHIM
The TRUE living God...My Creator
Do you know Him?

ABBA
My Father

ADONAI
The Lord...My master
Do you know Him?

EL ELYON
The Most High God...
He who is greater than any other god.
Do you know Him?

EL SHADDAI
The Almighty God
My supplier
Do you know Him?

EL OLAM
The Eternal God...He who is without ending
Do you know Him?
EL ROI
The God who sees me...
He watches me day and night, will never leave or forsake me.
Do you know Him?

EL GIBBOR
Mighty God...All Powerful
Do you Know Him?

EL EMETH
God of Truth
Do you know Him?

EL KANNA
Jealous God
Do you know Him?

EL MOSHAAH
God who Saves
Do you know Him?

YHWH SHAMMAH
The Lord is There.
Ever present with me, for His spirit lives in me.
Do you know Him?

YHWH SABAOTH
The Lord of Hosts.
God of heaven's Armies. My battles belong to Him.
Do you know Him?

YHWH TZIDKENU
The Righteous One.
He who keeps me in right-standing.
Do you know Him?

YHWH EL GMOLEH
God of recompense
He who will reward me.
Do you know Him?

YHWH YIREH
He who provides for me every day...
Do you know Him?

YHWH...NISSI
My Banner
He is my security, my hope, my freedom
Do you know Him?

YHWH SHALOM
He is my Peace
I have no need to be anxious
Do you know Him?

YHWH RAPHA
The Lord who heals.
He who repairs my body, binds up my emotional wounds and restores my joy, gives me beauty for ashes.
Do you know Him?

YHWH RO'EH
My Shepherd.
He who has restored my soul. He desires to be in relationship with me and I desire to be in relationship with Him.

Do you know Him?

YHWH M'KADEESHCHEM
My Sanctifier
He who makes me holy for I have been cleansed by the blood of the Lamb.
Do you know Him?

YHWH MEGAN
The Lord My Shield
Do you Know Him?

YHWH ORI
The Lord is My Light
Do you know Him?

YHWH UZZI
The Lord is My Strength
Do you know Him?

To think Lord, these are just a few of Your Names and attributes
Who is like unto You?
You are the undisputed heavy weight champion of the universe.
Even science cannot deny You
My Faith, My Hope, My Trust, is in You.
My Success is dependent upon You
My life is in Your Hands.

Thou shall have no other gods before me.
Exodus 20:3 KJV

MY CREATOR

Heavenly Father
Creator of the heaven and all that is upon the earth
I give You thanks
God of my salvation
The One who formed man from the dust
Blew life through the nostril of the still soil
Your breath circulating the interior of his emptiness
Transforming him into spirit and soul
I give You praise.

God of the universe
Whose word separated the seas from the dry land
Called the sun the moon and stars to come forth
Patterned the clouds with the mist of the morning dew
Coloured the rainbow with a reminder of Your promise
You who rotate the sequence of the seasons
I bow my heart in worship to You
For You are a great God.

God, my saviour, my shield and protector
The assessor of my inner being
He who looks at the condition of my heart
listens to the thoughts of my mind
The One who raises an eyebrow looking at me
Watching the movements of my feet and
the motions of my hands
Checking the integrity of my standing upon His provision,
the Rock
I surrender my all to You

Oh God of the heaven's armies I bless You
With all of my heart all of my mind and all the resources in me
For truly You are worthy of my praise
You and You alone are worthy of all earth's glory
Oh that men would indeed praise You
Oh that every living thing would praise You
Yes Lord, let everything that has life praise You
For Your mercies are from everlasting to everlasting.

Ah, Lord God! Behold! You have made the heavens
and the earth by Your great power and outstretched arm.
There is nothing too hard for You.
Jeremiah 32:17 NKJV

Often in my communication with My Lover & My King I just sit in wonderment of Him, reflecting on just how far He has brought me...a long, long way...

If it had not been the Lord on our side when people attacked us
Psalm 124:1 NIV

MY, my, my, if it had not been for You Lord, on my side. Bouy Sah! Who is like You? You're real! Yes You are! You're real, otherwise I'd probably be doing time. No one else could have caused the change in me like You; there is hope for everyone. You are hope. You will always be my HOPE! Indeed, You are the refining fire who is turning me into gold.

Thank You Lord
Thank Jesus, Yeshua
Love You loads
With all of my heart, all of my mind all of my soul.
I LOVE YOU!!!!!

Know, that I make NOOO apologies for my desire for My KING!
I am totally sold out for Him!

How precious are Your thoughts about me O God.
They cannot be numbered!
Psalm 37:17 NLT

Feed My Spirit!

Early one morning, walking out of my bedroom, I heard, "Feed My Spirit". It sounded like a strange request, because it was a season when I was praying and seeking the Lord. Next day, again I heard "Feed My Spirit"...I said "Lord what do you mean, *Feed My Spirit?* What do You want me to do," because I am praying. It felt as though the Holy Spirit was thirsty for my worship, He was hungry for more of me. It seemed like He was wanting me to visit heaven more; He was craving for me as much as I was yearning for Him. The more I made contact with Him through His word, is the more excited He appeared; we were both feasting together.

My goodness, I have had some experiences with the Holy Spirit that I cannot put into words because I just don't know how to explain it. What I do know is when we diligently seek the Lord, we will find Him. When we are sincere and devoted in prayer He responds in unfathomable ways, it just blows your mind if you try and work it out.

All seems a bit strange, I know!
Remember at the beginning of this journey, I shared how the Lord stopped me in my tracks to ask me why I was not showing up in His presence. Ask yourself, the same question...

"When was the last time I showed up properly in the throne room of heaven?"

I don't mean the little wishy washy prayer, flinging a cup of coffee down yuh throat rushing out the house, "o bless me Lord" prayer. I mean giving yourself some extra time in the mornings, getting out of you bed and penetrating the atmosphere with your call to your King.

I cannot remember where I heard this phase...

'Every time you call the name 'JESUS' He looks.'

If Jesus is attentively looking out for you, why aren't you showing up to greet Him in the morning? If you are, Brilliant!

I have learnt that the Holy Spirit in me is activated by food from the word of God and my thirst for Him. The more nourishment I give my spirit is the more I am sustained through my day.

Just turn back the page and look at His names and attributes. Recognise who it is that is keeping you. No educational institution, employer, celebrity, motivational or inspirational speaker, social media platform, no amount of likes, fame in the world or wealth gain, can give you the comfort, peace or satisfaction that you crave. The missing link in your life is an authentic relationship with God the Father...Lip service and having a form of godliness is not good enough. The Love of the King is joy unspeakable and full of glory. Only His presence in your life can position you for greatness. Success without the Holy Spirit is not soul satisfying. You may have the money, the bling bling and earthly luxuries, but there will always be a missing link; you cannot level up in life without Jesus.

I have learnt that the more the wealthy have, is the more they want, and some will go to any length, often causing others great pain, to get their feel-good currency. I have also learnt that rich people who achieve their wealth without integrity live their lives in dread, because they are always living in fear of loss. Jesus is the only one who gives complete mental satisfaction. His righteousness is real wealth and emotional security.

Today, call His Name, JESUS, JESUS, JESUS! Cause Him to look. Better still, if He stands at your door and knock...OPEN IT! Give Him reason to call you His friend and saturate you with His unfailing Love.

The song says;

What a friend we have Jesus!

My King, He is a friend indeed!

HE REALLY IS!

MY APPRECIATION

My God, My King, Lord and Saviour
I am so privileged to come before You today
In appreciation...I appreciate You
I am grateful for the opportunity to come before You
I love You, adore You
I bow my soul before You
Thank You for creating me for Your glory
Thank You for Your seed of greatness inside of me
Thank You for my installed gifts and potential
Thank You for the many life victories
waiting to burst forth
Today, Lord, let Your all-seeing eyes be
a torch to direct me to success
Let Your helping hands steady and
position me for favour
Guide me in all I do
By the power of my words I extract Your
blessings today
Instruct me by Your uprightness
Teach me how to show up in Your presence
The Psalmist pleaded with You,
"Lord teach me Your ways"
In his crave he said;
"Thy words I have hidden inside me that
I may not sin against You"
In my trying Lord, may I not displease You
See if there are any nasty ways in me
Expose my sins so they won't hold me captive
Wash me with Your spiritual hyssop
Cleanse me from all wrong intentions
Create in me correct motives and a right attitude

Lord show Yourself strong in my life
Uphold me with your right hand and allow me to be in right standing with You.
I present myself, my body, Your temple, to You (Mee), a living sacrifice
I give myself to You
Like Paul I die daily. I die to self today
Lord, yesterday has gone, today I need You
Lord, today I need Your anointing, to perfume my life and fragrance my day
Let Your sacred oil savour my path today
Let my lifestyle be a worshipping pleasure that makes You zealous over me
Let everything I do Lord be honest, governed by Your principles
Lord, let my life and everything I do bring You glory
Let my walk be a walk of certainty with virtue and without shame
Oh that Your hands will guide me to the open door of victory today
Again I ask Lord, position me to succeed
Let it be success that will demonstrate Your glory and change the unbelieving heart.
Thank You Lord for hearing me
In Jesus Name, Yeshua, I have prayed
Amen

I AM MY FATHER'S CHOICE

Before the foundation of the world
My love thought of you
Before I formed you in
Your mother's womb, I knew you
In the intimacy of passion
I guided sperm to egg
Among millions, My choice was you.
Fearfully and wonderfully I made you
In My image I created you
The very hairs on your head
I have numbered them
That's how much I love you.
In your body I breathed My Spirit
Evolving you into a living soul.
In your being I have imparted
Priceless gifting and talents.
In you the world will recognize
The beauty of My creativity
The awesomeness of My glory in you
will draw many souls to me
You are my outstanding joy bought by grace
I love you so much; I require much.
I the Lord have chosen you
O! How much I love you.
I...LOVE...YOU

"How precious is Your steadfast LOVE O God!
The children of mankind take refuge
in the shadow of Your wings."
Psalm 36:7

MY, MY, MY, MY
GLORRRY

MY GOD…MY KING

THANK YOUUUUU!

YOU KNOW MY NAME

I AM THE BREATH OF GOD!

RIGHT NOW FEELING YOUR FIRE LORD

NOBODY GREATER THAN
MY HEAVENLY DADDY

NOBODY!

NO COMPARISON TO MY CREATOR!

I Love the Book of Psalms.

Often, I use the Psalms to meditate and massage my heart. It is my go-to book when I feel low or stressed. I find the messages in the Psalms reassuring and a great way to talk to God and hear from Him. Thank God for King David, who many of the Psalms are credited to. In all honesty, I spent years believing David to be a real moany little man; he always appeared to be complaining to God about something. My feelings about him was that he should just man-up. However, after studying the bible more comprehensively, I changed my perception about him. I gained better understanding and a more in-depth insight of his character and his relationship with God.

Personal bible study takes you away from man's voice, to hearing God for yourself. My personal study of the word is what has brought me into relationship with Him acknowledging and embracing the scriptural verse...*And the Spirit of the Lord will rest on him; the Spirit of wisdom and understanding, the Spirit of counsel and might, the Spirit of knowledge and the fear of the Lord. Isaiah 1:3*. This was who David was. This was who Jesus was and is!

Studying the word of God, I discovered King David was everything but moany and miserable. Each Psalm depicts a particular crisis or situation he found himself him. His unique relationship with the Lord enabled him to write from his heart to his Father's heart. He not only knew his God but he knew the power of his divine protector. He knew where his help came from. He knew his God would never let him down. Perhaps the most fascinating thing I've found about King David was his desperation for his Lord, he was overwhelmingly passionate about His Heavenly Comforter. He looked to his God for all his needs. He enquired of Him in every aspect of his life, in kingship, in war, and most importantly in servitude.

God had such a niche relationship with David. Despite the fact he broke nearly every commandment, was an adulterer and murder, God declared him to be a man after His heart, and he was. David was a true worshipper in spirit and in truth. From childhood to death he was consumed with honouring his King with praise and worship. What I love most about King David is his loyalty, reverence to God and his sincere repentant heart.

I am absolutely fascinated by the relationship God had with David and in my spiritual opinion, it was due to his heart for worship, and I too have a heart for worship. I don't need to hear the preacher, really, I don't. Preaching is a bonus for me. I can either study the word for myself or ask Google. Thank God for technology; knowledge has increased. I need to worship. God needs worship.

In 2 Samuel 6:14-15 when the Ark of the Covenant returned to Israel, David danced before the Lord with all his might. So much so, he danced out of his royal garments. He was jumping and leaping. The people were shouting and sounding the trumpets and praising with their King. David did not care who despised him. Nothing or no one was going to stop him crazy praising his God. Likewise, I feel the same; don't tell me to be quiet when I'm praising my King. If you don't want to hear my praise, go home!

I Love You Lord. All of My Praise Belong to You!

BLESSED IS HE

Blessed is YHWH
The everlasting Father
God over all the earth
The King of kings
Whose authority rules the universe
And created all mankind in His image.

Blessed is the God of heaven
He who has no equal
He who has no rival
He who is subjected to no other power.
Blessed is He the righteous Judge, whose
salvation is sure
Blessed is the King Most High who
has made heaven His throne
He who sits on the foundation of
righteousness and justice
Blessed is He who has made the earth His footstool
He is ruler of everything and limitless
in His infinite wisdom.
Blessed is He who has no beginning
and is without ending
Blessed is He whose mercies endure forever
Great is His everlasting faithfulness.

Blessed is He the Great I AM
He who reigns supreme
Blessed is the One who was, just IS, and IS to come
Blessed is He the greatest manifestation of truth; pure and holy
Blessed is He who is devoted in the richness of compassion, He
never fails

Blessed is He whose gift of mercies are
waiting each morning
His all sufficient goodness and overflowing grace.

Blessed is He whose Holy Spirit is measureless
Blessed is He who cannot be compared to
Blessed is He who is worthy of our praise
Blessed is He the ever-present, all-knowing,
all-seeing God
Blessed is He the One who knows the
beginning from the ending.

Blessed is He who is unlimited in power
The one whose Spirit transcends the whole earth
Blessed is He who is able to forgive us
of our sins and set us free.
Blessed is He who is coming back again
In all His grandeur!
Blessed be My Lover and My King.

Bless the Lord O my soul and all that is within
me bless His Holy Name
Psalm 103:1KJV

Some years ago, 2004, when Joyce Myers visited the UK, NEC (Birmingham National Exhibition Centre), a friend and I decided to volunteer for counselling duties. On the first day of the seminar all the counsellors arrived early so we could be briefed before the meeting started. My friend went to find and secure our seats while I went along to the briefing session. For some reason during the briefing, I happen to look back and here comes my friend walking boldly down the aisle, strutting his stuff...three-piece suit, hair sleek with hair gel, bling bling shoes. He was the business. As he stood beside me, I burst into fits of laughter. I said...

"Michael, you overdid a bit didn't you." He took one look at me and pulling up his collar he replied, "Naa man, I didn't overdo it; I'm dressed for the King, Yu gatta look good for the King." It wasn't what Michael said, it was the way he said it; you knew there and then that he had a relationship with the King. When I thought about the title for this book, the Lord put me in remembrance of that moment.

I learnt from that experience that whatever I do in life I please God first. If He is pleased with my clothes, I am okay with that. If He is not pleased, I take it off. As much as is humanly possible for me, I will not intentionally do anything to offend God. I serve Him because He is souvenir and my life is all about Him.

Yes...My life is all about Him! It's taken me a long time to get here, but I'm here. The word of God tells us that God's people are destroyed for lack of knowledge...soo true...Let me just pause here for a moment and say***...Please take the time to study the word of God for yourself...***READ the bible. There are no mistakes. God is REAL His word is accurate...

When I consider all the years I have spent caught-up in church political foolishness, all because of my inadequate knowledge base. Not realising that all I simply had to do was what king Solomon did, ask God for wisdom, knowledge and understanding so I could fully manoeuvre my life according to His plan and purpose for me. When I first joined the church, the pastoral hierarchy was on such a pedestal, I thought only they were entitled to reach God. Let me be honest, I lived in fear of man rather than God. Yet the bible is clear, that the beginning of wisdom is the fear of God. And the fear of God is a healthy fear, not one that keeps you in bondage and distant from Him. The Lord wants us to draw close to Him in respect and reverential fear of who He is; He has a holy standard that we must adhere to. He has a love for us that is unimaginable. It seems almost illogical that someone would give up His most precious treasure for us. He fought a spiritual battle against the enemy and won...For you and for me... You don't learn this by just knowing about Him; you learn this by fervently searching for Him, finding Him, falling in love with Him and committing to Him with every fibre of your being.

At the start of my Christian journey it was so hellfire, brimstone and legalistic, I didn't realise I could have such an intimate relationship with God the Father; so much so I can now call Him my Lover and my King. When I first published this book in 2008, a Christian outlet refused to put the book in their shop window because they thought the title would cause offence. This is proof enough that a lot of God's people lack sound knowledge about who He is.

As my biblical understanding has increased, I have realised that the bible (from Genesis to Revelation), does not lie, even if as some say, there are missing books and misinformation, we have enough evidence to prove that our God exists. He is who He says He is, the I AM, and therefore, I have no excuse not to serve Him.

Thank You Lord for Your Word
Truly, the journey of the bible is the most
Romantic and Poetic Love Story!

ALL ABOUT HIM

It's forever about Him
All about Him
Everlastingly Him
Forgiveness is all about Him.
For ever and ever Him
My life is all about Him
Glory is all about him
My praise is all about Him
Grace is all about Him
My hope is all about Him.
Forever and forever
Mercy is all about Him
Ever, ever, ever and ever
Never endingly about Him
Throughout all eternity
All about Him
Not me, not you, not them
Just Him, Him, Him, Him, Him
Forever Him.
HIM!

"The son of man did not come to serve,
but to serve, and to give His life as a ransom for many"
(Matthews 20:28)

He Gave His Life for Me!

Thank You Lord...Bless Your Holy Name!
You still here?
Thank You!

You know from the minute we wake up our minds begin to wander. Our brains are extremely active and must find something to think about. I have developed a habit, where, before my mind begins searching for breakfast and finds some negative food, I feed it with thanksgiving, prayer and praise. I know my busy-body mind, so I bring it under subjection before it starts trying to take control. NO! *"I am not going to start the day with the news and the cares of the world".* I cannot afford to start my day in my feelings. I must make God my first priority as I awake, so He can manifest Himself in me and help me navigate my day. I cannot allow myself to do my day without the Holy Spirit...Do I trust my flesh?...NO...I need my Now and ever present God to help me grow in grace! After all, this is a two-way romance and I need Him more today than I needed Him yesterday and if He gives me breath for tomorrow, I will need Him more than I need today!

Finish praying and downstairs now!

I am ending this book, but feel as though I am just beginning. I could write so much more...I haven't reached...I am still learning...

Right now, I am tearfully sitting at my kitchen dining table looking through the patio doors. Again, I am contemplating on the goodness of God. I can't thank Him enough; Truly He is My Lover & My King.

I stop to fan, because it's that time of life. The Lord knows, I have gotten older but wiser and far more youthful in my soul than you could ever imagine. My spirit is alive, because He has come to life in me. It's a new day, a new dawning, a new life chapter for me; I have no words to fully explain, it's just how it is.

I look up again from my laptop and there goes the cat creeping along the fence, probably sneaking up to try and catch the squirrel. My garden is full of nature. It's a bright day, the rays of the sun are shining through the trees. There is a gentle breeze and the branches, are swaying; I believe they are giving praise to Adonai. I am watching the squirrel running across the grass, undetected by the cat, he's eating something; now he's digging, possibly searching for his nuts. Now he is on the fence staring at me through the door. He is just one of the many visiting garden personalities whose humorous characteristics bring joy and laughter to me every day.
In this moment, reflecting upon God's greatness and His astounding creativity, I consider Psalm 19:1...

"The heavens proclaim the glory of God. The skies display His craftsmanship."

I declare Your Glory Lord. I am Your prize possession crafted in Your Love.

I feel honoured
I am blessed, passionately favoured

No greater LOVE than the LOVER who laid down HIS LIFE for me!

This is a Heart wrenching God Moment!

I am thinking about one of the old-time songs that the elders used to sing at prayer meetings. It still makes my heart cry...

Heavenly Father I appreciate You
Heavenly Father I appreciate You
I love You adore You I bow down before You
Heavenly Father I appreciate You

Son of God I magnify You
Son of God I magnify You
You've saved me from sin sent the Holy Spirit within
Son of God I magnify You

Holy Spirit You are a comfort to me
Holy Spirit You are a comfort to me
You lead me You guide me, in danger You hide me
Holy Spirit You are a comfort to me.

Source: Hymns of Faith # 88
Author Anonymous...published 1977

Amen Amen and Amen...Glory to God! Lord I appreciate You.
YESSSSSSSSSS!
If you know the song sing it!
Believe me...This is a Tune!

CONNECTED TO MY KING!

Holy Father, my King
The One who sits high on His throne in the third heaven
The God who stretched out the universe
Whose footstool is earth
Your Royal Majesty
The supernatural One of great power
Holy is Your Name.
What a privilege and an honour, Lord, to be called by You
My heart is so glad that I ran to the door when You knocked
and opened my heart to Your offer of salvation
Your gift of love I could not refuse
You came in and have been resident since
My gratitude is never enough
Thank You!
You first loved me.

May I always be responsive to
YOU
May my mind never stop thinking about
YOU
May my heart never stop beating for
YOU
May my mouth never stop praising
YOU
May my eyes never stop seeing
YOUR GOODNESS
May my feet never stop walking in
YOUR PEACE
May my hands never grow weary
of being lifted up to
YOU

May my ears always be listening for
YOUR INSTRUCTIONS
May my soul always remain at rest in
YOUR ARMS
May my spirit always be receptive to
YOUR SPIRIT
May I always be mindful that my body is
YOUR TEMPLE
May my life always remain connected to
YOU

Abba my King hear my heart beat!
Love You with every strand of my being.

YHWH

God of heaven's Armies, Father, Creator and King
Indeed! I give You praise
Lord I exalt You
For You are the foundation of my life
I lift Your Name on High.
Yeshua, my Saviour, Mediator, Intercessor, my Hope
I magnify You
On Christ the solid ROCK I stand!
Holy Spirit my Comforter, Director, Way Maker, my Peace
I worship You
I glorify You
I bless Your Name
In You I put my trust to guide my footsteps
On the pathway of right standing.

YHWH
My God, my King
Hear my heart how it loves You
You are worthy of all my praise
I honour You with all of my whole being.
I give myself to You
I surrender all
Set Your seal of BLOOD upon my forehead
Make it plain to Your angelic host that...
I belong to You
I AM YOURS LORD!
My Soul...My Heart...My Mind are forever Yours.
Sincerely, YOU are...

MY LOVER & MY KING!

A Poetic Prayer of Praise

Now all glory to God, who is able to keep you from falling away and bring you with great joy into His glorious presence without a single fault. All glory to Him who alone is God, our Saviour, through Jesus Christ our Lord. All glory, majesty, power, and authority are His before all time, and in the present, and beyond, all time.

Amen.

Jude:24
Tree of Life Version.

Bless you for taking the time to journey the pathway of love with me. I know it has been an unusual journey, a bit quirky at times but I am a peculiar person. I hope travelling this winding road with me has given you some insight from my life experiences, challenges, my internal world of faith and my love for Christ. Hopefully, you found some similarities, maybe some answers, food for thought, laughter, and, or, some precious gems that will cause you to reflect on the goodness and greatness of God!

I have really appreciated and enjoyed your company and I hope the next time we meet it will be you taking me on your journey with Your Lover & Your King!

One last piece of advice - Stay close to Abba; seek Him with all of your heart, all your soul and all your strength. He is right there waiting!

The Lord bless you and keep you; the Lord make His face shine on you and be gracious to you; the Lord turn His face towards you and give you peace.

Numbers 6:24-26 NIV

SHALOM!

Printed in Great Britain
by Amazon

61448566R00128